# PRAISE FOR
## *THE ART OF CLEAN CODE*

"An excellent book packed full of insights that every programmer (and project manager) should know."

—TIM COX, AUTHOR OF *RASPBERRY PI COOKBOOK FOR PYTHON PROGRAMMERS*

"An extremely readable book . . . Readers of this book will likely come away as believers in a more minimalistic mindset. Moreover, the book lives up to its title. The lessons taught can be applied not only in coding but also toward making the reader's life generally more productive and successful."

—LEE TESCHLER, MICROCONTROLLER TIPS

"A great source to learn about the basic principles of clean code and best practices to get better at coding . . . Reading this book saves you time and teaches valuable skills, so go for it!"

—CROW INTELLIGENCE

"I very much enjoyed [*The Art of Clean Code*], and definitely would recommend it to anybody, not just programmers or related, but anybody, as it does apply to nearly everyone, if they can think outside the box!"

—LUKAS BATEMA, FOUNDER OF BATEMADEVELOPMENT

# THE ART OF CLEAN CODE

## BEST PRACTICES TO ELIMINATE COMPLEXITY AND SIMPLIFY YOUR LIFE

by Christian Mayer

**no starch press®**

San Francisco

Printed in the United States of America

Second printing

28 27 26 25 24    2 3 4 5 6

ISBN-13: 978-1-7185-0218-5 (print)
ISBN-13: 978-1-7185-0219-2 (ebook)

 Published by No Starch Press®, Inc.
245 8th Street, San Francisco, CA 94103
phone: +1.415.863.9900
www.nostarch.com; info@nostarch.com

Publisher: William Pollock
Production Manager: Rachel Monaghan
Production Editor: Katrina Taylor
Developmental Editor: Liz Chadwick
Cover Illustrator: Gina Redman
Interior Design: Octopod Studios
Technical Reviewer: Noah Spahn
Copyeditor: Sadie Barry
Compositor: Jeff Lytle, Happenstance Type-O-Rama
Proofreader: Paula L. Fleming, Fleming Editorial Services
Indexer: BIM Creatives, Inc.

Library of Congress Control Number: 2022932408

For customer service inquiries, please contact info@nostarch.com. For information on distribution, bulk sales, corporate sales, or translations: sales@nostarch.com. For permission to translate this work: rights@nostarch.com. To report counterfeit copies or piracy: counterfeit@nostarch.com.

*To my kids, Amalie and Gabriel*

## About the Author

Christian Mayer is the founder of the popular Python site Finxter.com, an educational platform that helps teach more than five million people a year how to program. He has a PhD in computer science and has published a number of books, including *Python One-Liners* (No Starch Press, 2020), *Leaving the Rat Race with Python* (2021), and the Coffee Break Python series.

## About the Technical Reviewer

Noah Spahn has a wide-ranging background in software engineering. He has a master's degree in software engineering from California State University, Fullerton, and currently works in the Computer Security Group at the University of California, Santa Barbara (UCSB). Noah has taught Python courses at the UCSB Interdisciplinary Collaboratory and an upper division course on the Concepts of Programming Languages at Westmont College. Noah is glad to teach anyone who is interested in learning.

# BRIEF CONTENTS

# CONTENTS IN DETAIL

# 4
# WRITE CLEAN AND SIMPLE CODE     51

# 5
# PREMATURE OPTIMIZATION IS THE ROOT OF ALL EVIL     79

# 9
# FOCUS
**135**

# FOREWORD

I remember how excited I was when I learned my first line of Python code; it was like I had just entered a whole new universe of magical powers. As time passed, I learned to manipulate Python variables, lists, and dictionaries. Then I learned to write Python functions and enthusiastically started writing more complex Python code. But it didn't take me long to realize that writing code did not make me a skillful programmer—it was as if I had just learned a few magic tricks but was very far from becoming a programming wizard.

Although it got the job done, my code was dreadful: repetitive and hard to read. When Chris told me about this book, I thought to myself *I wish I had this book when I first started coding.* There are plenty of books that teach you the technicalities of coding, but books like *The Art of Clean Code* are rare. This book will show you how to apply nine principles to improve your programming competence. And good programming skills lead to cleaner code, greater focus, more effective use of your time, and higher quality results.

Reading about "How Complexity Harms Your Productivity" (Chapter 1) would have been very helpful to me as I was learning Python and data visualization, because I would have realized early on that I could build powerful dashboards with less code that's easier to read. When I was first starting, as I learned more Python functions and operations, I just wanted to use all these new magical tricks to build formidable data visualizations. But then I learned to build them with cleaner code instead of just using new tricks, and debugging my code became infinitely simpler and faster.

The state of flow and the Unix philosophy, covered in Chapters 6 and 7, were two additional principles I wish I had known years ago. Multitasking is a capability that our culture tends to see as a desirable skill. I was often proud of my ability to code while paying attention to my email and phone. It took me a while to realize how impactful it could be to shut down distractions and dedicate my attention solely to the piece of code at hand. A few months later, I started blocking out time on my calendar to focus on coding. Not only did I end up writing better code with fewer errors, but I also got much more enjoyment out of the process.

By applying the principles described in this book, you shorten the path to becoming a skillful programmer. In fact, I have had the opportunity to witness firsthand the benefits of applying the book's principles: Chris's code is clean, his writing is compelling, and he is prolific. I consider myself fortunate to have worked with Chris and to have seen how he embodies the principles that he emphasizes in this book.

Knowing how to code well requires curiosity and practice. However, there is a difference between a good coder and a good programmer—this book will help you become a good programmer who is more focused, more productive, and more effective.

Adam Schroeder, Community Manager at Plotly
Co-author of *Python Dash* (No Starch Press, 2022)

# ACKNOWLEDGMENTS

Putting together a programming book builds on the ideas and contributions of a multitude of people. Rather than trying to list them all, I want to follow my own advice: *less is more*.

First and foremost, I want to thank you. I've written this book for you to help you improve your coding skills and solve practical problems in the real world. For trusting me with your valuable time, I'm grateful. My primary goal with this book is to make it worth your while by sharing tips and strategies to save you time and reduce your stress throughout your coding career.

My greatest source of motivation came from the active members of the Finxter community. Every day, I get encouraging messages from Finxter students that motivate me to keep producing content.

My deep gratitude goes to the No Starch Press team for making the book-writing process such an enlightening experience. I want to thank my editor, Liz Chadwick; it's because of her outstanding lead that the book reached a level of clarity I wouldn't be able to pull off myself. Katrina Taylor carried the book from draft to publication with a rare talent for people management and textual understanding. Thanks for making the book real, Katrina! My technical reviewer, Noah Spahn, invested his excellent technical skills to "debug my writing." Special thanks to No Starch Press's founder, Bill Pollock, for allowing me to contribute in a small way—with yet another book alongside *Python One-Liners* and *Python Dash*—to his mission to educate and entertain coders. Bill is an inspiring and sought-after leader in the coding industry, yet he still finds the time to do the small things, such as responding to my messages and questions during holidays, weekends, and nights!

I'm forever grateful to my beautiful and supportive wife, Anna; my lovely daughter, Amalie, who is full of fantastic stories and ideas; and my curious son, Gabriel, who never fails to make everybody around him happier.

And with that, let's get started, shall we?

# INTRODUCTION

Once upon a time, Bill Gates' parents invited legendary investor Warren Buffett to the family home to spend some time together.

In a CNBC interview, Warren Buffett recounts how on this occasion, Bill's father asked Warren and Bill to write down the secrets of their success. I'll tell you in a moment what they wrote.

At the time, the tech prodigy Bill Gates had met the famous investor Buffett only once or twice, but they had become fast friends, both leading successful billion-dollar companies. The young Bill Gates was on the verge of achieving his mission of placing a *computer on every desk* with his fast-growing software giant Microsoft. Warren Buffett had made his name as one of the most successful business geniuses in the world. Famously, Warren had grown his majority-owned company, Berkshire Hathaway, from a broke textile manufacturer to an international heavyweight in diversified business areas such as insurance, transportation, and energy.

So, what did those two business legends consider the secret of their success? As the story goes, without any collaboration, Bill and Warren each wrote down a single word: *Focus.*

**NOTE** *You can watch Warren Buffett discussing the interaction in an interview on CNBC in a YouTube clip entitled "'One word that accounted for Bill Gates' and my success: Focus' — Warren Buffett."*

While this "success secret" sounds simple enough, you may wonder: Does it apply to my career as a coder too? What does focus look like in practice—coding through the night with energy drinks and pizza, or perhaps eating an all-protein diet and getting up at sunrise? What are the not-so-obvious consequences of leading a focused life? And, importantly, are there actionable tips on how a programmer like me can benefit from the abstract principle to increase my productivity?

This book aims to answer these questions to help you lead a more focused life as a programmer and become more effective in your daily work. I'll show you how you can increase your productivity by writing clean, concise, and focused code that is easier to read, write, and collaborate on with other programmers. As I'll show you in the upcoming chapters, the focusing principle holds in every stage of software development; you'll learn how to write clean code, create focused functions that do one thing well, create fast and responsive applications, design focused user interfaces for usability and aesthetics, and plan product roadmaps using minimum viable products. I'll even show you how achieving a pure state of focus can vastly increase your concentration and help you experience more excitement and joy from your tasks. As you'll see, the overarching theme of this book is to focus in every way you can—I'll show you exactly how to do this in the upcoming chapters.

For any serious coder, continuous improvement of your focus and productivity is essential. When you do more valuable work, you tend to get greater rewards. However, simply increasing your output is not the solution. The trap goes like this: *if I write more code, create more tests, read more books, learn more, think more, communicate more, and meet more people, I'll get more done.* But you cannot do *more* without doing something *less.* Time is limited—you have 24 hours per day and 7 days a week, just like me and everybody else. There's an inescapable mathematical limitation: in a limited space, if one thing grows, something else must shrink to make room. If you read more books, you may meet fewer people. If you meet more people, you may write less code. If you write more code, you may have less time with the people you love. You cannot escape the fundamental trade-off: there cannot be *more* without *less* in a limited space.

Rather than focus on the obvious consequence of simply doing more, this book takes the reverse perspective: you reduce complexity, allowing you to work less while getting more value from your results. Thoughtful minimalism is the holy grail of personal productivity, and, as you'll see in later chapters, it works. You can create more value with fewer resources by programming computers the right way and using the timeless principles presented in this book.

By creating more value, you can also command higher pay. Bill Gates famously said that a "great lathe operator commands several times the wage of an average lathe operator, but a great writer of software code is worth 10,000 times the price of an average software writer."

One reason is that a great software developer performs a highly leveraged activity: programming a computer the right way can replace thousands of jobs and millions of hours of paid work. Code that runs self-driving cars, for example, can replace the labor of millions of human drivers while being cheaper, more reliable, and (arguably) much safer.

## Who Is This Book For?

Are you a coding practitioner who wants to create more value with faster code and less pain? Do you ever find yourself stuck in bug-finding mode? Does the complexity of code often overwhelm you? Do you struggle to decide on the next thing to learn, having to choose from hundreds of programming languages—Python, Java, C++, HTML, CSS, JavaScript—and thousands of frameworks and technologies—Android apps, Bootstrap, TensorFlow, NumPy? If you can answer any of the questions with "YES!" (or even "yes"), you have the right book in your hands!

This book is for every programmer who's interested in increasing their productivity—doing more with less. It's for you if you seek simplicity and believe in Occam's razor: "It is futile to do with more things that which can be done with fewer."

## What Will You Learn?

This book shows you how to practically apply nine principles to increase your potential as a programmer by orders of magnitude. These principles will simplify your life and reduce complexity, struggles, and working hours. I don't claim that any of the principles are new. They're variously well known and established—and proven to work by the most successful coders, engineers, philosophers, and creators. That's what makes them principles in the first place! However, in this book I will apply the principles explicitly to coders, giving real-world examples and, where possible, code examples.

**Chapter 1** will set up the main challenge to increasing value in productivity: complexity. You'll learn to recognize the sources of complexity in your life and your code and gain an understanding that complexity can harm your productivity and output. Complexity is everywhere, and you need to be constantly vigilant against it. *Keep it simple!*

In **Chapter 2**, you'll learn the profound impact the *80/20 principle* can have on your life as a programmer. The majority of effects (80 percent) come from a minority of causes (20 percent); this is a ubiquitous theme in programming. You'll learn that the 80/20 principle is fractal: 20 percent of the 20 percent of coders will earn 80 percent of the 80 percent of salary. In other words, 4 percent of the world's coders earn 64 percent of the money. The quest for continuous leverage and optimization is always on!

In **Chapter 3**, you'll learn about *building minimal viable products* to test your assumptions early, minimize waste, and increase the speed by which you go through the build, measure, and learn cycle. The idea is to learn where to focus your energy and attention by getting feedback early.

In **Chapter 4**, you'll learn about the benefits of *writing clean and simple code*. Contrary to what most people intuitively assume, code should be written, first and foremost, to maximize readability rather than minimize the usage of central processing unit (CPU) cycles. Collective programmer time and effort are far scarcer than CPU cycles, and writing code that's hard to grasp reduces the efficiency of your organization—and of our collective human intelligence.

In **Chapter 5**, you'll learn about the conceptual foundation of performance optimization and the pitfalls of optimizing prematurely. Donald Knuth, one of the fathers of computer science, used to say, *"Premature optimization is the root of all evil!"* When you do need to optimize your code, use the 80/20 principle: optimize the 20 percent of functions that run 80 percent of the time. Get rid of the bottlenecks. Ignore the rest. Repeat.

In **Chapter 6**, you'll join me for an excursion into Mihaly Csikszentmihalyi's (literally) exciting world of *flow*. The state of flow is a state of pure concentration that increases productivity by magnitudes and helps to build a culture around deep work—speaking in the words of computer science professor Cal Newport, who also lends some ideas to this chapter.

In **Chapter 7**, you'll learn about the Unix philosophy of *doing one thing* and doing it well. Rather than having a monolithic (and, potentially, more efficient) kernel with a huge provision of functionality, the developers of Unix chose to implement a small kernel with lots of optional helper functions. This helped the Unix ecosystem to scale up while remaining clean and (relatively) simple. We'll see how you can apply these principles to your own work.

In **Chapter 8**, you'll enter another vital area in computer science that benefits from a minimalistic mindset: design and user experience (UX). Think of the differences between Yahoo Search and Google Search, the Blackberry and the iPhone, and OkCupid and Tinder. The most successful technologies often come with a radically simple user interface for the reason that, in design, *less is more*.

In **Chapter 9**, you'll revisit the power of *focus* and learn how to apply it in diverse areas to increase your (and your programs') output vastly!

Finally, we'll wrap things up, give you actionable next steps, and release you into the complex world equipped with a set of reliable tools to simplify that world.

# 1

## HOW COMPLEXITY HARMS YOUR PRODUCTIVITY

In this chapter, we're going to have a comprehensive look at the important and highly underexplored topic of complexity. What exactly is *complexity*? Where does it occur? How does it damage your productivity? Complexity is the enemy of the lean and efficient organization and individual, so it's worth taking a close look at all areas where we find complexity and what forms it takes. This chapter focuses on the problem—complexity—and the remaining chapters will explore effective methods to attack it by redirecting the released resources previously occupied by complexity.

Let's start with a quick overview of where complexity may be daunting to a new coder:

- Choosing a programming language
- Choosing a coding project to work on—from thousands of open source projects and myriads of problems

- Deciding which libraries to use (scikit-learn versus NumPy versus TensorFlow)
- Deciding which emerging technologies to invest time in—Alexa apps, smartphone apps, browser-based web apps, integrated Facebook or WeChat apps, virtual reality apps
- Choosing a coding editor such as PyCharm, Integrated Development and Learning Environment (IDLE), and Atom

Given the great confusion caused by these sources of complexity, it's no surprise that *"How do I start?"* is one of the most common questions from programming beginners.

The best way to start is *not* by choosing a programming book and reading about all the syntactical features of the programming language. Many ambitious students buy programming books as an incentive and then add the learning task to their to-do lists—if they've spent money on the book, they better read it or the investment will be lost. But as with so many other tasks on to-do lists, *reading a programming book* is seldomly completed.

The best way to start is to choose a practical code project—a simple one if you're a beginner—and push it to completion. Don't read coding books or random tutorials on the web before completing a full project. Don't scroll through endless feeds on StackOverflow. Just set up the project and start coding with the limited skills you have and your common sense. A student of mine wanted to create a financial dashboard application checking the historic returns of different asset allocations to answer questions such as "What was the maximum down year of a portfolio consisting of 50 percent stocks and 50 percent government bonds?" At first she didn't know how to approach this project but soon found out about a framework called Python Dash that deals with building data-based web apps. She learned how to set up a server and studied just the HyperText Markup Language (HTML) and Cascading Style Sheets (CSS) she needed to move forward, and now her app is live and has already helped thousands of people find the right asset allocation. But, more importantly, she joined the team of developers that created Python Dash and is even writing a book about it with No Starch Press. She did all of this in one year—and you can, too. It's okay if you don't understand what you're doing; you will gradually increase your understanding. Read articles only to make progress on the project in front of you. The process of finishing your first project introduces a number of highly relevant problems, including:

Which code editor should you use?

How do you install your project's programming language?

How do you read input from a file?

How do you store the input in your program for later use?

How do you manipulate the input to obtain the desired output?

By answering these questions, you'll gradually build a well-rounded skill set. Over time, you'll be able to answer these questions better and more easily. You'll be able to solve much bigger problems, and you'll build up an internal database of programming patterns and conceptual insights. Even advanced coders learn and improve with this same process—only the coding projects have become much larger and more complicated.

With this project-based learning approach, you'll likely find that you struggle with complexity in areas such as finding bugs in ever-growing codebases, understanding code components and how they interact, choosing the right feature to be implemented next, and understanding the mathematical and conceptual basics of the code.

Complexity is everywhere, at every stage of a project. The hidden cost of this complexity is often that brand-new coders throw in the towel and their projects never see the light of day. So, the question arises: How do I solve the problem of complexity?

The answer is straightforward: *simplicity*. Seek simplicity and focus in every stage of the coding cycle. If you take only one thing away from this book, let it be this: take a radically minimalistic position in every area you encounter in programming. Throughout the book, we'll discuss all of the following methods:

- Declutter your day, do fewer tasks, and focus your efforts on the tasks that matter. For example, instead of starting 10 new interesting code projects in parallel, carefully select one and focus all your efforts on finishing this one project. In Chapter 2, you'll learn about the 80/20 principle in programming in greater detail.

- Given one software project, strip away all unnecessary features and focus on the minimum viable product (see Chapter 3), ship it, and validate your hypotheses quickly and efficiently.

- Write simple and concise code wherever you can. In Chapter 4, you'll learn many practical tips for how to accomplish this.

- Reduce time and effort spent on premature optimization—optimizing code without need is one of the major reasons for unnecessary complexity (see Chapter 5).

- Reduce switching time by blocking large chunks of time for programming to obtain a state of *flow*—a term from psychological research to describe a focused state of mind that increases your attention, focus, and productivity. Chapter 6 is all about reaching a state of flow.

- Apply the Unix philosophy of focusing code functions on one objective only ("Do One Thing Well"). See Chapter 7 for a detailed guide to the Unix philosophy with Python code examples.

- Apply simplicity in design to create beautiful, clean, and focused user interfaces that are easy to use and intuitive (see Chapter 8).

- Apply focusing techniques when planning your career, your next project, your day, or your area of expertise (see Chapter 9).

Let's dive deeper into the concept of complexity to develop an understanding of one of the great enemies of your coding productivity.

## What Is Complexity?

In different fields, the term *complexity* comes with different meanings. Sometimes, it's strictly defined, such as the *computational complexity* of a computer program that provides a means to analyze a given code function for varying inputs. Other times, it's loosely defined as the amount or structure of interactions between system components. In this book, we're going to use it more generically.

We'll define *complexity* as follows:

**Complexity**   A whole, made up of parts, that is difficult to analyze, understand, or explain.

Complexity describes a whole system or entity. Because complexity makes the system difficult to explain, complexity causes struggle and confusion. Because real-world systems are messy, you'll find complexity everywhere: the stock market, social trends, emerging political viewpoints, and big computer programs with hundreds of thousands of lines of code—such as the Windows operating system.

If you're a coder, you are especially prone to overwhelming complexity, such as from these different sources that we'll cover in this chapter:

Complexity in a project life cycle

Complexity in software and algorithmic theory

Complexity in learning

Complexity in processes

Complexity in social networks

Complexity in your daily life

## Complexity in a Project Life Cycle

Let's dive into the different stages of the project life cycle: planning, defining, designing, building, testing, and deployment (see Figure 1-1).

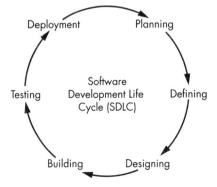

Figure 1-1: The six conceptual phases of
a software project based on the official
Institute of Electrical and Electronics Engineers
(IEEE) standard for software engineering

Even if you're working on a very small software project, you're likely going through all six phases of the software development life cycle. Note that you may not necessarily go through each phase only once—in modern software development, a more iterative approach is generally preferred where each phase is revisited multiple times. Next, we'll look at how complexity has a significant impact on each phase.

## Planning

The first stage of the software development life cycle is the planning phase, sometimes known in engineering literature as *requirement analysis*. The purpose of this phase is to determine how the product will look. A successful planning phase leads to a strictly defined set of required features to deliver to the end user.

Whether you're a single person working on your hobby project or you're responsible for managing and orchestrating collaboration among multiple software development teams, you must figure out the optimal set of features of the software. A number of factors must be taken into consideration: the costs of building a feature, the risk of not being able to successfully implement the feature, the expected value for the end user, marketing and sales implications, maintainability, scalability, legal restrictions, and many more.

This phase is crucial because it can save you from wasting massive amounts of energy later. Planning mistakes can lead to millions of dollars' worth of wasted resources. On the other hand, careful planning can set the business up for great success in the years to follow. The planning phase is a time to apply your newly acquired skill of 80/20 thinking (see Chapter 2).

The planning phase is also difficult to do right because of the complexity involved. Several considerations add to the complexity: assessing risk properly in advance, figuring out the strategic direction of a company or an organization, guessing the customers' responses, weighing the positive impact of different feature candidates, and determining the legal implications of a given software feature. Taken together, the sheer complexity of solving this multidimensional problem is killing us.

## Defining

The defining phase consists of translating the results from the planning phase into properly specified software requirements. In other words, it formalizes the output of the previous phase to gain approval or feedback from clients and end users who will later use the product.

If you've spent a lot of time planning and figuring out the project requirements but fail in communicating them well, it'll cause significant problems and difficulties later. A wrongly specified requirement that helps the project may be just as bad as a correctly formulated requirement that doesn't. Effective communication and precise specification are crucial to avoid ambiguities and misunderstandings. In all human communication, getting your message across is a highly complex endeavor due to the "curse of knowledge" and other psychological biases that outweigh the relevance of personal experiences. If you try to deliver ideas (or requirements for that matter) out of your head and into another one's head, be careful: complexity is out to get you!

### Designing

The goal of the designing phase is to draft the architecture of the system, decide on the modules and components that deliver the defined functionality, and design the user interface—while keeping the requirements developed in the previous two phases in mind. The gold standard of the designing phase is to create a crystal-clear picture of how the final software product will look and how it's built. This holds for all methods of software engineering. Agile approaches would just iterate over those phases more quickly.

But the devil lies in the detail! A great system designer must know about the pros and cons of a huge variety of software tools they may use to build the system. For example, some libraries may be easy for the programmer to use but slow in execution speed. Building custom libraries is harder for the programmers but may result in much higher speed and, consequently, improved usability of the final software product. The designing phase must fix these variables so that the benefit-to-cost ratio is maximized.

### Building

The building phase is where many coders want to spend all their time. This is where the transformation from the architectural draft to the software product happens. Your ideas transform into tangible results.

Through proper preparation in the previous phases, a lot of complexity has already been eliminated. Ideally, the builders should know which features to implement from all the possible features, how the features look, and which tools to use to implement them. Yet, the building phase is always full of new and emerging problems. Unexpected things like bugs in external libraries, performance issues, corrupted data, and human mistakes can slow progress. Building a software product is a highly complicated endeavor. A small spelling mistake can undermine viability of the whole software product.

### Testing

Congratulations! You've implemented all requested features, and the program seems to work. You're not done yet, though. You still must test the behavior of your software product for different user inputs and usage patterns. This phase is often the most important of all—so much so that many practitioners now advocate the use of *test-driven development* where you don't even start to implement (in the building phase) without having written all tests. While you can argue against that point of view, it's generally a good idea to spend time testing your product by creating test cases and checking if the software delivers the correct result for these test cases.

For example, say you're implementing a self-driving car. You must write *unit tests* to check that each little function (a *unit*) in your code generates the desired output for a given input. Unit tests will usually uncover some faulty functions that behave strangely under certain (extreme) inputs. For example, consider the following Python function stub that calculates the average red, green, and blue (RGB) color value of an image, perhaps used to differentiate whether you're traveling through a city or a forest:

```
def average_rgb(pixels):
    r = [x[0] for x in pixels]
    g = [x[1] for x in pixels]
    b = [x[2] for x in pixels]
    n = len(r)
    return (sum(r)/n, sum(g)/n, sum(b)/n)
```

For example, the following list of pixels will yield the average red, green, and blue values of 96.0, 64.0, and 11.0, respectively:

```
print(average_rgb([(0, 0, 0),
                   (256, 128, 0),
                   (32, 64, 33)]))
```

Here's the output:

```
(96.0, 64.0, 11.0)
```

Although the function seems simple enough, many things can go wrong in practice. What if the pixel list of tuples is corrupted and some (RGB) tuples have only two instead of three elements? What if one value is of a non-integer type? What if the output must be a tuple of integers to avoid the floating-point error that is inherent to all floating-point computations?

A unit test can test for all of those conditions to make sure that the function works in isolation.

Here are two simple unit tests, one that checks whether the function works for a border case with zeros as inputs and another that checks whether the function returns a tuple of integers:

```
def unit_test_avg():
    print('Test average...')
    print(average_rgb([(0, 0, 0)]) == average_rgb([(0, 0, 0), (0, 0, 0)]))

def unit_test_type():
    print('Test type...')
    for i in range(3):
        print(type(average_rgb([(1, 2, 3), (4, 5, 6)])[i]) == int)

unit_test_avg()
unit_test_type()
```

The result shows that the type check fails and the function doesn't return the correct type, which should be tuple-of-integer values:

```
Test average...
True
Test type...
```

```
False
False
False
```

In a more realistic setting, testers would write hundreds of those unit tests to check the function against all types of inputs—and whether it generates the expected outputs. Only if the unit tests reveal that the function works properly can we move on to test higher-level functions of the application.

In fact, even if all your unit tests successfully pass, you haven't yet completed the testing phase. You must test the correct interaction of the units as they're building a greater whole. You must design real-world tests, driving the car for thousands or even tens of thousands of miles to uncover unexpected behavior patterns under strange and unpredictable situations. What if your car drives on a small road without road signs? What if the car in front of you abruptly stops? What if multiple cars wait for each other at a crossroad? What if the driver suddenly steers into approaching traffic?

There are so many tests to consider; the complexity is so high that many people throw in the towel here. What looked good in theory, even after your first implementation, often fails in practice after applying different levels of software testing such as unit tests or real-world usage tests.

### Deployment

The software has now passed the rigorous testing phase. It's time to deploy it! Deployment can take many forms. Apps may be published to marketplaces, packages may be published to repositories, and major (or minor) releases may be made public. In a more iterative and agile approach to software development, you revisit the deployment phase multiple times using *continuous deployment*. Depending on your concrete project, this phase requires you to launch the product, create marketing campaigns, talk to early users of the product, fix new bugs that will surely come to light after being exposed to users, orchestrate the deployment of the software on different operating systems, support and troubleshoot different kinds of problems, or maintain the codebase to adapt and improve over time. This phase can become quite messy, given the complexity and interdependency of the various design choices you made and implemented in previous phases. The subsequent chapters will suggest tactics to help you overcome the mess.

## Complexity in Software and Algorithmic Theory

There can be as much complexity *within* a piece of software as there is in the process that surrounds software development. Many metrics in software engineering measure the complexity of software in a formal way.

First, we'll look at *algorithmic complexity*, which is concerned with the resource requirements of different algorithms. Using algorithmic complexity, you can compare different algorithms that solve the same problem. For example, say you've implemented a game application with a high-score rating system. You want the players with the highest scores to appear at the top of the list and the players with the lowest scores to appear at the bottom. In other words, you need to *sort* the list. Thousands of algorithms exist for sorting a list, and sorting a list is computationally more demanding for 1,000,000 players than it is for 100 players. Some algorithms scale better with increasing size of the list input; others scale worse. While your app serves a few hundred users, it doesn't really matter which algorithm you choose, but as your user base grows, the runtime complexity of the list grows superlinearly. Soon, the end users will have to wait longer and longer for the list to be sorted. They'll start complaining, and you'll need better algorithms!

Figure 1-2 exemplifies the algorithmic complexity of two schematic algorithms. The x-axis shows the size of the list to be sorted. The y-axis shows the runtime of the algorithm (in time units). Algorithm 1 is much slower than Algorithm 2. In fact, the inefficiency of Algorithm 1 becomes more apparent the more list elements must be sorted. Using Algorithm 1, your game app would become slower the more users are playing.

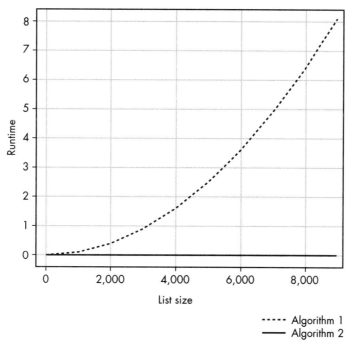

Figure 1-2: Algorithmic complexity of two different sorting algorithms

Let's see whether this holds for real Python sorting routines. Figure 1-3 compares three popular sorting algorithms: bubble sort, Quicksort, and Timsort. Bubble sort has the highest algorithmic complexity. Quicksort and Timsort have the same asymptotical algorithmic complexity. But the Timsort algorithm is still much faster—that's why it's used as Python's default sorting routine. The runtime of the bubble sort algorithm explodes with a growing list size.

In Figure 1-4, we repeat this experiment but only for Quicksort and Timsort. Again, there's a drastic difference in algorithmic complexity: Timsort scales better and is faster for the growing list size. Now you see why Python's built-in sorting algorithm hasn't changed for such a long time!

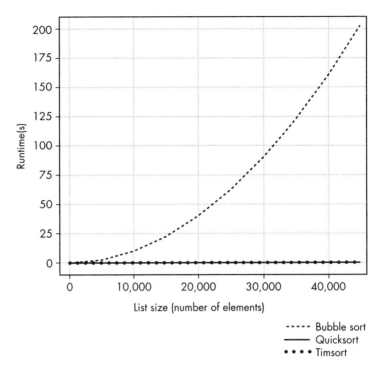

Figure 1-3: Algorithmic complexity of bubble sort, Quicksort, and Timsort

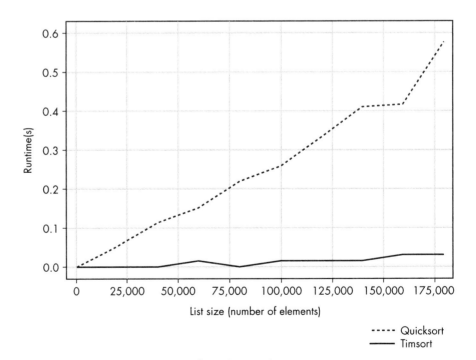

Figure 1-4: Algorithmic complexity of Quicksort and Timsort

Listing 1-1 shows the code in Python in case you want to reproduce the experiment. I'd recommend you choose a smaller value for n because the code runs a long time on my machine before terminating.

```python
import matplotlib.pyplot as plt
import math
import time
import random


def bubblesort(l):
    # src: https://blog.finxter.com/daily-python-puzzle-bubble-sort/
    lst = l[:] # Work with a copy, don't modify the original
    for passesLeft in range(len(lst)-1, 0, -1):
        for i in range(passesLeft):
            if lst[i] > lst[i + 1]:
                lst[i], lst[i + 1] = lst[i + 1], lst[i]
    return lst


def qsort(lst):
    # Explanation: https://blog.finxter.com/python-one-line-quicksort/
    q = lambda lst: q([x for x in lst[1:] if x <= lst[0]])
                    + [lst[0]]
                    + q([x for x in lst if x > lst[0]]) if lst else []
    return q(lst)


def timsort(l):
    # sorted() uses Timsort internally
    return sorted(l)


def create_random_list(n):
    return random.sample(range(n), n)




n = 50000
xs = list(range(1,n,n//10))
y_bubble = []
y_qsort = []
y_tim = []

for x in xs:

    # Create list
    lst = create_random_list(x)

    # Measure time bubble sort
    start = time.time()
```

```
bubblesort(lst)
y_bubble.append(time.time()-start)

# Measure time qsort
start = time.time()
qsort(lst)
y_qsort.append(time.time()-start)

# Measure time Timsort
start = time.time()
timsort(lst)
y_tim.append(time.time()-start)


plt.plot(xs, y_bubble, '-x', label='Bubblesort')
plt.plot(xs, y_qsort, '-o', label='Quicksort')
plt.plot(xs, y_tim, '--.', label='Timsort')

plt.grid()
plt.xlabel('List Size (No. Elements)')
plt.ylabel('Runtime (s)')
plt.legend()
plt.savefig('alg_complexity_new.pdf')
plt.savefig('alg_complexity_new.jpg')
plt.show()
```

*Listing 1-1: Measuring elapsed runtime for three popular sorting routines*

Algorithmic complexity is a thoroughly researched field. In my opinion, the improved algorithms produced from this research are among the most valuable technological assets of humanity, allowing us to solve the same problems with fewer resources, over and over. We truly stand on the shoulders of giants.

In addition to algorithmic complexity, we can measure the complexity of code with *cyclomatic complexity*. This metric, developed by Thomas McCabe in 1976, describes the number of *linearly independent paths* through your code, or the number of paths that have at least one edge that's not in another path. For example, code with an if statement would result in two independent paths through your code, so it would have a higher cyclomatic complexity than flat code without any branching like that in an if statement. Figure 1-5 shows the cyclomatic complexity of two Python programs that process user input and respond accordingly. The first program contains only one conditional branch, which could be considered a fork in the road. Either branch could be taken, but not both. Thus, the cyclomatic complexity is two because there are two linearly independent paths. The second program contains two conditional branches leading to a total of three linearly independent paths and a cyclomatic complexity of three. Each additional if statement increases cyclomatic complexity.

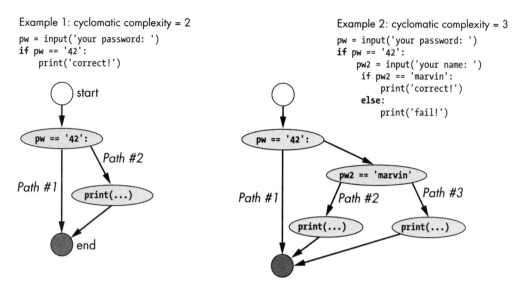

Example 1: cyclomatic complexity = 2
```
pw = input('your password: ')
if pw == '42':
    print('correct!')
```

Example 2: cyclomatic complexity = 3
```
pw = input('your password: ')
if pw == '42':
    pw2 = input('your name: ')
    if pw2 == 'marvin':
        print('correct!')
    else:
        print('fail!')
```

*Figure 1-5: Cyclomatic complexity of two Python programs*

The cyclomatic complexity is a solid proxy metric for the hard-to-measure *cognitive complexity*, that is, how difficult it is to understand a given codebase. However, cyclomatic complexity ignores the cognitive complexity that comes from, say, multiple nested for loops compared to a flat for loop. That's why other measures such as NPath complexity improve upon cyclomatic complexity. To sum up, code complexity not only is an important subject of algorithmic theory but also is relevant for all practical matters when implementing code—and for writing easy-to-understand, readable, and robust code. Both algorithmic theory and programming complexity have been thoroughly researched for decades. A primary goal of these efforts is to *reduce computational and non-computational complexity* to mitigate its harmful effects on productivity and resource utilization of humans and machines alike.

## Complexity in Learning

Facts don't exist in a vacuum but are interrelated. Consider these two facts:

Walt Disney was born in the year 1901.

Louis Armstrong was born in the year 1901.

If you fed a program with these facts, it could answer questions like *"What's the birth year of Walt Disney?"* as well as questions like *"Who was born in 1901?"* To answer the latter, the program must figure out the interdependency of different facts. It may model the information like this:

```
(Walt Disney, born, 1901)
(Louis Armstrong, born, 1901)
```

To get all persons born in 1901, it could use the query (*, born, 1901) or any other way to relate the facts and group them together.

In 2012, Google launched a new search feature showing info boxes on the search result page. These fact-based info boxes are populated using a data structure called the *knowledge graph*, which is a massive database of billions of interrelated facts to represent information in a network-like structure. Instead of storing objective and independent facts, this database maintains information about the interrelationship between different facts and other pieces of information. The Google search engine uses this knowledge graph to enrich its search results with higher-level knowledge and form answers autonomously.

Figure 1-6 shows an example. One node on the knowledge graph may be about the famous computer scientist Alan Turing. In the knowledge graph, the concept of Alan Turing is connected to different pieces of information such as his birth year (1912), his fields of study (Computer science, Philosophy, Linguistics), and his doctoral advisor (Alonzo Church). Each of those pieces of information is also connected to other facts (Alonzo Church's field of study was Computer science as well), forming a massive network of interrelated facts. You can use this network to acquire new information and answer user queries programmatically. A query about the "field of study of Turing's doctoral advisor" would result in the deducted answer "Computer science". While this may sound trivial or obvious, the ability to generate new factoids like these has led to a breakthrough in information retrieval and search engine relevancy. You'd probably agree that it's far more effective to learn by association than by remembering unrelated facts.

```
Some triples represented in the graph:
("Alan Turing", "has doctoral advisor", "Alonzo Church")
("Alan Turing", "has field of study", "Philosophy")
("Alan Turing", "has field of study", "Linguistics")
```

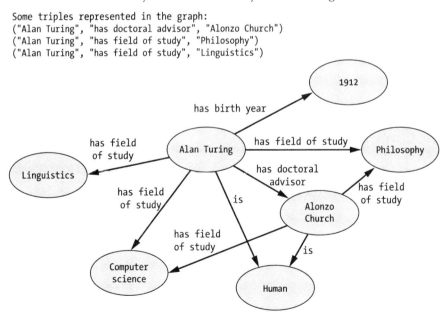

*Figure 1-6: Knowledge graph representations*

Every field of study focuses only on a small part of the graph, each consisting of myriads of interrelated factoids. You can only really understand a field by taking into account related facts. To understand Alan Turing thoroughly, you must research his beliefs, his philosophies, and the characteristics of his doctorate advisor. To understand Church, you must investigate his relationship to Turing. Of course, there are too many related dependencies and facts in the graph to expect to understand everything. The complexity of these interrelations imposes the most fundamental boundaries around your ambitions to learn. Learning and complexity are two sides of the same coin: complexity is at the boundary of the knowledge you've already acquired. To learn more, you must first know how to control complexity.

We're getting kind of abstract here, so let's have an example! Say you want to program a trading bot that buys and sells assets according to a set of sophisticated rules. You could learn lots of useful knowledge before starting your project: the basics of programming, distributed systems, databases, application programming interfaces (APIs), web services, machine learning, and data science and the related mathematics. You could learn about practical tools such as Python, NumPy, scikit-learn, ccxt, TensorFlow, and Flask. You could learn about trading strategies and stock market philosophies. Many people approach these problems with such a mindset and so never feel ready to start the project. The problem is that the more you learn, the less knowledgeable you feel. You'll never attain sufficient mastery in all those fields to truly satisfy your desire to feel prepared. Overwhelmed by the complexity of the whole endeavor, you feel like quitting. Complexity is about to take its next victim: you.

Fortunately, in the chapters of this book, you'll learn skills to combat complexity: focus, simplification, scaling down, reduction, and minimalism. This book will teach you those skills.

## Complexity in Processes

A *process* is a series of actions taken with the goal of realizing a defined result. The complexity of a process is calculated by its number of actions, participants, or branches. In general, the more actions (and participants), the more complicated a process becomes (see Figure 1-7).

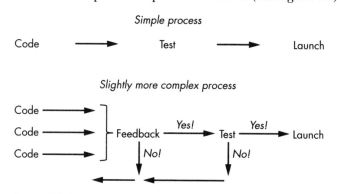

Figure 1-7: Two example processes: one-person development versus team development

Many software companies follow process models for different aspects of the business in an attempt to simplify processes. Here are some examples:

Software development may use agile development or scrum.

Customer relationship development may use customer relationship management (CRM) and sales scripts.

New product and business model creation may use the business model canvas.

When organizations accumulate too many processes, complexity starts to clog the system. For example, before Uber entered the scene, the process of traveling from location A to B often involved many steps: finding telephone numbers of taxi organizations, comparing rates, preparing different payment options, and planning different modes of transportation. For many, Uber streamlined the process of traveling from A to B, integrating the whole planning process into an easy-to-use mobile application. The radical simplification performed by Uber made traveling more convenient for customers and reduced planning time and costs compared to the traditional taxi industry.

In overly complex organizations, innovation finds fewer vehicles for change because it's unable to break through the complexity. Resources are wasted as actions within processes become redundant. Trying to fix the suffering business, managers invest energy in establishing new processes and new actions, and the vicious cycle begins to destroy the business or organization.

Complexity is the enemy of efficiency. The solution here is minimalism: to keep your processes efficient, you must radically weed out unnecessary steps and actions. It's very unlikely that you'll find your processes *oversimplified*.

## Complexity in Your Daily Life, or Death by a Thousand Cuts

The purpose of this book is to increase the productivity of your programming efforts. Your progress can be interrupted by your own personal daily habits and routines. You must tackle the daily distractions and the constant competition for your valuable time. Computer science professor Cal Newport talks about this in his excellent book *Deep Work: Rules for Focused Success in a Distracted World* (Grand Central Publishing, 2016). He argues that there's both an *increasing* demand for work that requires deep thinking—such as programming, researching, medicine, and writing—and a *decreasing* supply of time to do it due to the proliferation of communication devices and entertainment systems. If increasing demand meets decreasing supply, economic theory suggests that prices will rise. If you are capable of engaging in deep work, your economic value will increase. There has never been a better time for programmers who can engage in deep work.

Now, the caveat: it has become almost impossible to engage in deep work if you don't brutally enforce its prioritization. The external world is a nonstop distraction. Your colleagues pop into your office. Your smartphone demands your attention every 20 minutes. Your inbox pops up a new email dozens of times a day—each asking for a slice of your time.

Deep work results in delayed gratification; it's a satisfying feeling to have spent weeks of work on a computer program and find that it works. However, what you *desire* in most moments is instant gratification. Your subconscious often looks for ways to escape from the effort of deep work. Small rewards produce an easy boost of endorphins: checking your messages, engaging in meaningless chitchat, flicking through Netflix. The promise of delayed gratification becomes less and less attractive compared to the happy, colorful, and lively world of instant gratification.

Your efforts to stay focused and productive are prone to dying the death of a thousand cuts. Yes, you can turn off your smartphone once and use willpower to avoid checking your social media and switching on your favorite shows, but can you do it consistently day after day? Here, too, the answer lies in applying radical minimalism to the root of the problem: *uninstall* social media apps rather than trying to manage consumption, *reduce* the number of projects and tasks you're involved in rather than trying to do more by working more, *go deep* into one programming language rather than spending lots of time switching between many.

## Conclusion

By now, you should be thoroughly motivated by the need to overcome complexity. For further exploration of complexity and how we might overcome it, I do recommend reading *Deep Work* by Cal Newport.

Complexity harms productivity and reduces focus. If you don't take early control over complexity, it will quickly consume your most precious resource: time. At the end of your life, you won't judge whether you've led a meaningful life based on how many emails you've replied to, hours of computer games you've played, or Sudoku puzzles you've solved. By learning how to handle complexity, by keeping it simple, you'll be able to fight complexity and give yourself a powerful competitive advantage.

In Chapter 2, you'll learn about the power of the 80/20 principle: focus on the vital few and ignore the trivial many.

# 2

## THE 80/20 PRINCIPLE

In this chapter, you'll learn about the profound impact of the *80/20 principle* on your life as a programmer. It has many names, including the *Pareto principle*, named after its discoverer Vilfredo Pareto. So, how does the principle work, and why should you care? The 80/20 principle refers to the idea that a majority of effects (80 percent) come from a minority of causes (20 percent). It shows you a path to achieve many more results as a professional coder by focusing your efforts on a few important things and ignoring the many things that hardly move the needle.

### 80/20 Principle Basics

The principle says that the majority of effects come from the minority of causes. For example, the majority of income is earned by the minority of people, the majority of innovations come from the minority of researchers, the majority of books are written by the minority of authors, and so on.

You may have heard about the 80/20 principle—it's everywhere in personal productivity literature. The reason for its popularity is twofold. First, the principle allows you to be relaxed and productive at the same time as long as you can figure out the things that matter, which make up the 20 percent of activities that lead to 80 percent of the results, and focus on those relentlessly. Second, we can observe the principle in a huge variety of situations, giving it considerable credibility. It's even tough to come up with a counterexample, where the effects come equally from the causes. Try to find some examples of 50/50 distributions where 50 percent of the effects come from 50 percent of causes! Sure, the distribution is not always 80/20—the concrete numbers can change to 70/30, 90/10, or even 95/5— but the distribution is always heavily skewed toward the minority producing the majority of effects.

We represent the Pareto principle with a Pareto distribution, shown in Figure 2-1.

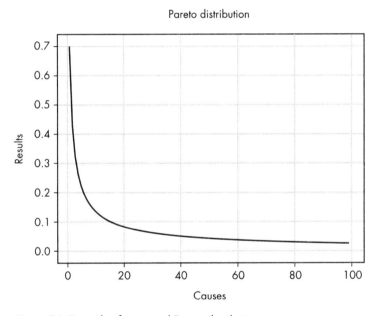

*Figure 2-1: Example of a general Pareto distribution*

The Pareto distribution plots the results (y-axis) against the causes (x-axis). The results can be any measure of success or failure, like income, productivity, or the number of bugs in a software project. The causes can be any entity these results may be associated with, such as employees, businesses, or software projects, respectively. To obtain the characteristic Pareto curve, we order the causes according to the results they produce. For example, the person with the highest income comes first on the x-axis, then comes the person with the second-highest income, and so on.

Let's look at a practical example.

## Application Software Optimization

Figure 2-2 shows the Pareto principle in action in an imaginary software project: the minority of the code is responsible for the majority of the runtime. The x-axis shows code functions sorted by the runtime they incur. The y-axis shows the runtime of those code functions. The shaded area that dominates the overall area under the plot shows that most code functions contribute much less to the overall runtime than a few selected code functions. Joseph Juran, one of the early discoverers of the Pareto principle, calls the latter the *vital few* and the former the *trivial many*. Spending a lot of time optimizing the trivial many barely improves the overall runtime. The existence of Pareto distributions in software projects is well supported by scientific evidence such as in "Power Laws in Software" by Louridas, Spinellis, and Vlachos (2008).

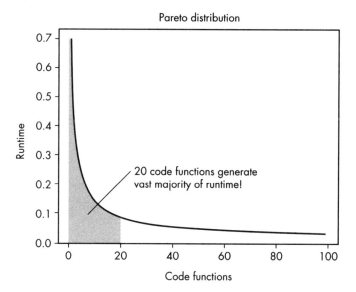

*Figure 2-2: Example of a Pareto distribution in software engineering*

Large companies like IBM, Microsoft, and Apple employ the Pareto principle to build faster, more user-friendly computers by channeling their focus on the vital few, that is, by repeatedly optimizing the 20 percent of the code that was executed most often by the average user. Not all code is created equal. A minority of code has a dominating impact on the user experience, while much of the code has little impact. You might double-click the File Explorer icon multiple times per day, but you seldom change the access rights of a file. The 80/20 principle tells you where to focus your optimization efforts!

The principle is easy to understand, but it can be harder to know how you can use the principle in your own life.

# Productivity

By focusing on the vital few rather than the trivial many, you can increase your productivity by a factor of 10, even 100. Don't believe me? Let's calculate where these numbers come from, assuming an underlying 80/20 distribution.

We'll use the conservative 80/20 parameters (80 percent of the results come from 20 percent of the people) and then calculate the rate of production for each group. In some fields (like programming), the distribution is probably much more skewed.

Figure 2-3 shows that in a company of 10 employees, just 2 employees produce 80 percent of the results, while 8 employees produce 20 percent of the results. We divide 80 percent by 2 employees for an average output of 40 percent per top-performing employee in the company. If we divide the 20 percent of the results generated by the 8 employees, we get an average of 2.5 percent of output per bottom-performing employee. The difference in performance is 16 times!

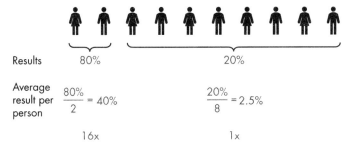

Figure 2-3: The average output of the top 20 percent of performers is 16 times the average output of the bottom 80 percent.

This 16-times difference in average performance is a fact in millions of organizations throughout the world. The Pareto distribution is also fractal, which means that the top 20 percent of the top 20 percent generate 80 percent of 80 percent of the results, accounting for even more significant performance differences in large organizations with thousands of employees.

The differences in results cannot be explained by intelligence alone—a person cannot be 1,000 times more intelligent than another person. Instead, the differences in results come from the specific behavior of the individual or the organization. If you did the same things, you could get the same results. However, before you change your behavior, you must be clear about what result you want to accomplish, as research shows an extreme inequality of results in almost any metric you can imagine.

**Income**   Ten percent of the people earn almost 50 percent of the income in the United States.

**Happiness**   Less than 25 percent of the people in North America rate their happiness a 9 or 10 on a 0–10 scale where "the worst possible life" is a 0 and "the best possible life" is a 10.

**Monthly active users**   Just 2 out of the top 10 websites intended for all audiences get 48 percent of the cumulative traffic, as shown in Table 2-1 (based on information from *https://www.ahrefs.com/*).

**Book sales**   Just 20 percent of authors may receive as much as 97 percent of sales.

**Scientific productivity**   For example, 5.2 percent of scientists account for 38 percent of published articles.

The resources section at the end of the chapter links to some articles to support this data. The inequality of results is a well-established phenomenon in social science, and it is commonly measured in a metric called the *Gini coefficient*.

**Table 2-1:** Cumulative Traffic of the 10 Most-Trafficked Websites in the United States

| # | Domain | Monthly traffic | Cumulative |
|---|--------|-----------------|------------|
| 1 | en.wikipedia.org | 1,134,008,294 | 26% |
| 2 | youtube.com | 935,537,251 | 48% |
| 3 | amazon.com | 585,497,848 | 62% |
| 4 | facebook.com | 467,339,001 | 72% |
| 5 | twitter.com | 285,460,434 | 79% |
| 6 | fandom.com | 228,808,284 | 84% |
| 7 | pinterest.com | 203,270,264 | 89% |
| 8 | imdb.com | 168,810,268 | 93% |
| 9 | reddit.com | 166,277,100 | 97% |
| 10 | yelp.com | 139,979,616 | 100% |
| | | 4,314,988,360 | |

So how can you become one of the top performers? Or, to formulate it more generally: How can you *move to the left* on the Pareto distribution curve in your organization (see Figure 2-4)?

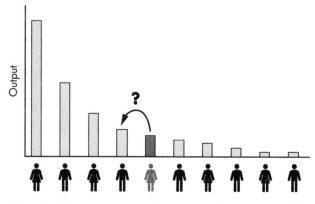

*Figure 2-4: To create more output, you need to move to the left of the curve.*

## Success Metrics

Let's say you want to optimize for income. How can you move to the left on the Pareto curve? We're leaving exact science behind here, because you need to find the reasons some people succeed in your specific industry and develop actionable success metrics you can control and implement. We define the term *success metrics* as measurements of the behaviors that lead to more success in your field. The tricky thing is that the most crucial success metrics are different in most fields. The 80/20 principle also applies to success metrics: some success metrics have a large impact on your performance in a field, while others barely matter at all.

For example, when working as a doctoral researcher, I soon realized that success was all about getting cited by other researchers. The more citations you have as a researcher, the more credibility, visibility, and opportunities you'll have. However, *increasing the number of citations* is hardly an actionable success metric that you can optimize daily. The number of citations is a *lagging indicator*, because it is based on actions you took in the past. The problem with lagging indicators is that they record only the consequence of past actions. They don't tell you the right actions to take daily for success.

To obtain a measure for doing the right actions, the notion of leading indicators was introduced. A *leading indicator* is a metric that predicts a change in the lagging indicator before it occurs. If you do more of the leading indicator, the lagging indicator is likely to improve as a result. As a researcher, then, you'll receive more citations (lagging indicator) by publishing more high-quality research papers (leading indicator). That means writing high-quality papers is the most important activity for most scientists, not secondary activities such as preparing presentations, organizing, teaching, or drinking coffee. The success metric for researchers is therefore generating a maximal number of high-quality papers, as shown in Figure 2-5.

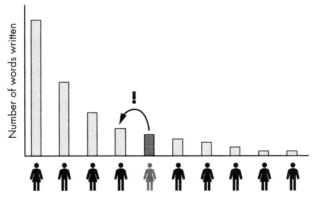

*Figure 2-5: Success metric in research: number of words written to produce a high-quality paper*

To push to the left in research, you must write more words today, publish your next high-quality paper sooner, receive more citations faster, grow your scientific footprint, and become a more successful scientist. Roughly speaking, many different success metrics can serve as a proxy for "being successful in science." For instance, when ordering them on a scale from lagging to leading measures, you may get *number of citations, number of high-quality papers written, number of total words written in your life,* and *number of words written today.*

The 80/20 approach allows you to identify the activities on which you must focus. Doing more of the success metrics, preferably actionable lead measures, will increase your professional success, and that's all that should matter. Spend less time on all the other tasks. Refuse to die the death of a thousand cuts. Be lazy with all activities but one: *writing more words per day.*

Say you work 8 hours per day and you divide your day into eight 1-hour activities. After completing the success metric exercise, you realize that you can skip two 1-hour activities per day and complete four other activities in half the time by being less perfectionistic. You have saved 4 hours per day, but you still accomplish 80 percent of your results. Now you can invest 2 hours into writing more words for high-quality papers per day. Within a few months, you'll have submitted an extra paper, and over time, you'll submit more papers than any of your colleagues. You work only 6 hours per day, and you generate imperfect quality in most of your work tasks. But you shine where it matters: you submit more research papers than anyone else in your environment. As a result, you'll soon be one of the top 20 percent of researchers. You generate more with less.

Instead of becoming a "Jack of all trades, master of none," you gain expertise in the area that is most important to you. You heavily focus on the vital few and ignore the trivial many. You lead a less stressful life, but you enjoy more fruits from your invested labor, efforts, time, and money.

## Focus and the Pareto Distribution

A closely related topic I want to discuss is *focus.* We'll discuss focus in many places in this book—for example, Chapter 9 discusses the power of focus in detail—but the 80/20 principle explains *why* focus is so powerful. Let's dive into the argument!

Consider the Pareto distribution in Figure 2-6 that shows the percentage improvement of moving toward the top of the distribution. Alice is the fifth most productive person in the organization. If she overtakes just one person in the organization, thereby becoming the fourth most productive person, she'd increase her output (salary) by 10 percent. One step further than that, and her output increases by an *additional* 20 percent. In a Pareto distribution, the growth per rank explodes exponentially, so even small increases in productivity can result in big increases in income. Increasing your productivity leads to superlinear improvements in your income, happiness, and joy at work. Some call this phenomenon "the winner takes all."

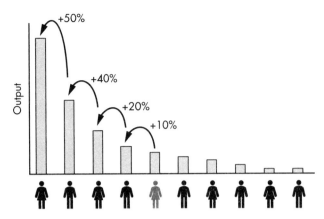

Figure 2-6: Disproportional benefit of improving your rank in a Pareto distribution

That's why it doesn't pay to spread your attention: *if you don't focus, you participate in many Pareto distributions.* Consider Figure 2-7: Alice and Bob can each invest three units of learning effort every day. Alice focuses on one thing: programming. She spends her three units of effort on learning to code. Bob spreads his focus across multiple disciplines: one unit of time polishing his chess skills, one unit improving his programming skills, and one unit improving his political skills. He's reached average skill and output in each of the three areas. But the Pareto distribution disproportionally rewards the top performers, so Alice collects more total output reward.

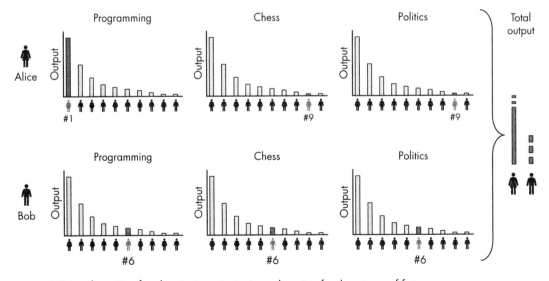

Figure 2-7: Nonlinearity of rank output—a strategic explanation for the power of focus

The disproportional rewards hold within each area, too. For instance, Bob may spend his time reading three general books (let's call them

*Introduction to Python*, *Introduction to C++*, and *Introduction to Java*) while Alice reads three books diving deep into machine learning with Python (let's call them *Introduction to Python*, *Introduction to Machine Learning with Python*, and *Machine Learning for Experts*). As a result, Alice will focus on becoming a machine learning expert and can demand a higher salary for her specialized skill set.

## Implications for Coders

In programming, the results tend to be much more heavily skewed toward the top than in most other fields. Instead of 80/20, the distribution often looks more like 90/10 or 95/5. Bill Gates said a *"great lathe operator commands several times the wage of an average lathe operator, but a great writer of software code is worth 10,000 times the price of an average software writer."* Gates argues that the difference between a great and an average software writer is not 16 times, but 10,000 times! Here are several reasons why the software world is prone to such extreme Pareto distributions:

- A great programmer can solve some problems that the average programmer simply cannot solve. In some instances, this makes them infinitely times more productive.

- A great programmer can write code that is 10,000 times faster than the code of an average programmer.

- A great programmer writes code with fewer bugs. Think about the effect of a single security bug on Microsoft's reputation and brand! Moreover, every additional bug costs time, energy, and money for subsequent modifications of the codebase and feature additions—the detrimental, compounding effect of bugs.

- A great programmer writes code that is easier to extend, which may improve the productivity of thousands of developers that work on the code at a later stage of the software development process.

- A great programmer thinks out of the box and finds creative solutions to circumvent costly development efforts and help focus on the most important things.

In practice, a combination of these factors is at play, so the difference can be even higher.

So, for you, the key question may be this: How do you become a great programmer?

### A Success Metric for Programmers

Unfortunately, the statement "become a great programmer" is not a success metric you can directly optimize—the problem is multidimensional. A great programmer understands code quickly, knows algorithms and data structures, knows different technologies and their strengths and weaknesses, can collaborate with other people, is communicative and creative, stays educated and knows about ways to organize the software development process, and possesses hundreds of soft and hard skills. But you can't be a master of all of those! If you don't focus on the vital few, you'll become washed away by the trivial many. To become a great programmer, you must focus on the vital few.

One of the vital few activities to focus on is to write more lines of code. The more lines you write, the better coder you'll become. It's a simplification of the multidimensional problem: by optimizing the proxy metric (write more lines of code), you increase your odds of success at the target metric (become a great writer of software code). See Figure 2-8.

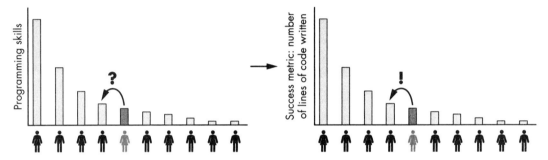

Figure 2-8: Success metric in programming: number of lines of code written

By writing more code, you'll understand code better, and you'll talk and behave more like an expert coder. You'll attract better coders to your network and find more challenging programming tasks, so you'll write even more code and become even better. You'll get paid more and more per line of code you write. You or your company can outsource the trivial many tasks.

Here's an 80/20 activity you can follow every day: track the number of lines you code every day and optimize it. Make it a game to at least match your average every day.

## Pareto Distributions in the Real World

We'll take a quick look at some real-world examples of the Pareto distribution in action.

### GitHub Repository TensorFlow Contributions

We can see an extreme example of a Pareto distribution in contributions to GitHub repositories. Let's consider a wildly popular repository for machine learning computations in Python: *TensorFlow*. Figure 2-9 shows the top seven contributors to this GitHub repository. Table 2-2 shows the same data numerically.

GitHub TensorFlow Repository Commits

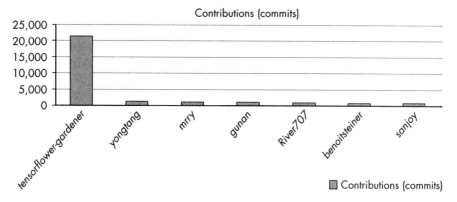

Figure 2-9: GitHub TensorFlow repository commit distribution

**Table 2-2:** Number of TensorFlow
Commits and Their Contributors

| Contributor | Commits |
| --- | --- |
| tensorflower-gardener | 21,426 |
| yongtang | 1,251 |
| mrry | 1,120 |
| gunan | 1,091 |
| River707 | 868 |
| benoitsteiner | 838 |
| sanjoy | 795 |

The user *tensorflow-gardener* contributed more than 20 percent of the 93,000 commits to this repository. Given that there are thousands of contributors, the distribution is much more extreme than the 80/20 distribution. The reason is that the contributor *tensorflow-gardener* consists of the team of coders at Google that created and maintains this repository. Yet, even when this team is filtered out, the remaining individual top contributors are hugely successful programmers with impressive track records. You can check them out on the public GitHub page. Many of them have landed exciting jobs working for very attractive companies. Whether they became successful before or after they generated a large number of commits to the open source repository is a merely theoretical discussion. For all practical purposes, you should start your success habit: write more lines of code every day now. Nothing is stopping you from becoming number two on the TensorFlow repository—by committing valuable code to the TensorFlow repository two to three times per day for the next two to three years. If you persist, you can join the ranks of the most successful coders on earth just by choosing one powerful habit and sticking to it for a few short years!

## Programmer Net Worth

Sure enough, the net worth of programmers is also Pareto distributed. For privacy reasons, it's hard to get data about an individual's net worth, but the website *https://www.networthshare.com/* does show the self-reported net worth of various professions, including programmers. The data is a bit noisy, but it shows the idiosyncratic skewness of real-world Pareto distributions (Figure 2-10).

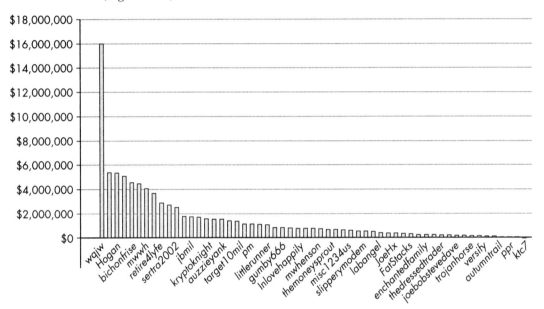

*Figure 2-10: Self-reported net worth of 60 programmers*

Quite a few software millionaires in our small sample of 29 data points! But the curve is likely to be even more skewed in the real world because there are also many billionaire programmers—Mark Zuckerberg, Bill Gates, Elon Musk, and Steve Wozniak come to mind. Each of those tech geniuses created the prototypes of their services themselves, laying a hand on the source code. Lately, we've seen many more of those software zillionaires in the blockchain space.

## Freelance Gigs

The freelance developing space is dominated by two marketplaces where freelancers can offer their services and clients can hire freelancers: Upwork and Fiverr. Both platforms grow double digits per year in terms of users and revenues, and both platforms are committed to disrupting the organization of the world's talents.

The average income of a freelance developer is $51 per hour. But this is only the average rate—the top 10 percent of freelance developers earn much higher hourly rates. In more or less open markets, income resembles a Pareto distribution.

I have observed this skewed income distribution in my own experience from three perspectives: (1) as a freelancer, (2) as a client hiring hundreds of freelancers, and (3) as a course creator offering Python freelancing education. Most students fail to reach even the average earning potential because they don't stay in the game for more than a month or so. The ones who keep working on their freelancing business daily for several months usually reach the average $51 per hour earning target. A minority of very ambitious and dedicated students reach $100 per hour and more.

But why do some students fail while others thrive? Let's plot the number of successful gigs completed by freelance developers on the Fiverr platform with an average rating of at least 4 out of 5. I focused on the popular area of machine learning in Figure 2-11. I collected the data from the Fiverr website and tracked the number of completed gigs for 71 freelancers on the two top search results for the category Machine Learning Gigs. Not surprisingly, for us, the distribution resembles a Pareto distribution.

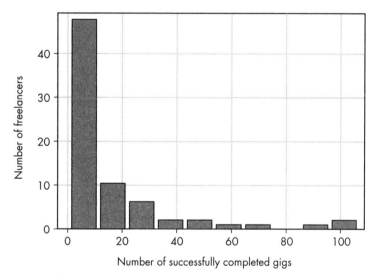

Figure 2-11: Histogram of Fiverr freelancers and the number of gigs they completed

From my own experience as a teacher of thousands of freelancing students, I'm fascinated to see that the vast majority of students have completed fewer than 10 gigs. I'm pretty sure that many of those students will later proclaim, "Freelancing doesn't work." To me, this statement is an oxymoron like "work doesn't work" or "business doesn't work." These freelancing students fail because they don't try hard and long enough. They assume that they can make money easily, and when they realize that they must work persistently to join the freelancing winners, they're quick to give up.

This lack of freelancing persistence actually provides an excellent opportunity for you to move up the Pareto distribution. The simple success metric that virtually ensures you eventually join the top 1–3 percent of freelancers is this: *complete more gigs*. Stay in the game longer. Anyone can do this. The fact that you're reading this book shows that you have the commitment, ambition, and motivation to become a top 1–3 percent freelance coding professional. Most players suffer from a lack of focus, and even if they are skilled, intelligent, and well connected, they have no chance of competing against a focused, dedicated, and Pareto-knowledgeable programmer.

## Pareto Is Fractal

The Pareto distribution is fractal. If you zoom in, observing only a part of the whole distribution, there's another Pareto distribution! This works as long as the data is not too sparse; in that case, it loses its fractal nature. A single data point, for example, cannot be considered a Pareto distribution. Let's look at this property in Figure 2-12.

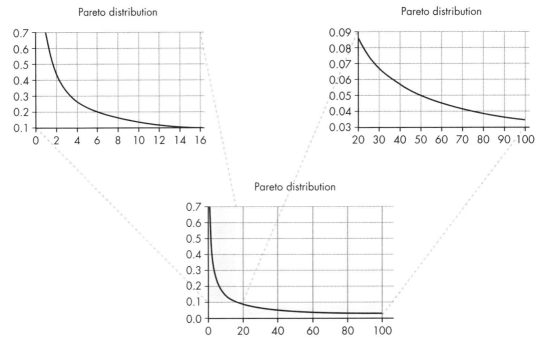

Figure 2-12: The fractal nature of a Pareto distribution

In the center of Figure 2-12 is the Pareto distribution from Figure 2-1. I used the simple Python script in Listing 2-1 to zoom into this Pareto distribution:

```
import numpy as np
import matplotlib.pyplot as plt

alpha = 0.7

x = np.arange(100)
y = alpha * x / x**(alpha+1)
```

```
plt.plot(x, y)

plt.grid()
plt.title('Pareto Distribution')
plt.show()
```

*Listing 2-1: An interactive script for you to zoom into a Pareto distribution*

You can play with the code yourself; just copy it into your Python shell and run the code. If you do this in your Python shell, you'll be able to zoom into different areas of the Pareto distribution.

The Pareto distribution has various practical applications in life and programming, and I'll discuss some of them in this book, but, in my experience, the most transformative application for you will be to become an *80/20 thinker*; that is, you constantly try to find ways to accomplish much more with much less. Please note that while the concrete Pareto numbers—80/20, 70/30, or 90/10—may vary in your own life, you may draw some value from the fractal nature of productivity and output distributions. For instance, it is always true that not only do a few programmers earn much more than the rest but also a few of those top earners earn more than the rest of the top earners. The pattern stops only when the data gets too sparse. Here are some examples:

**Income**   Twenty percent of the top 20 percent of coders will earn 80 percent of the 80 percent of income. In other words, 4 percent of the coders will earn 64 percent of the income! This implies that you're never stuck with your current financial situation, even if you already belong to the top 20 percent of coders. (This paper is just one of many that show the fractal nature of income distributions: *http://journalarticle.ukm.my/ 12411/1/29%20Fatimah%20Abdul%20Razak.pdf.*)

**Activities**   Twenty percent of the most impactful 20 percent of the most impactful 20 percent of the activities you have done this week are often responsible for 80 percent of the 80 percent of the 80 percent of your results. In this scenario, 0.8 percent of the activities will lead to 51 percent of the results. Roughly speaking, if you're working 40 hours per week, 20 minutes may account for half of the results in your workweek! An example of such a 20-minute activity would be writing a script that automates a business task and saves you a couple of hours every few weeks that you can invest in other activities. If you're a programmer, deciding to skip the implementation of an unnecessary feature can save you tens of hours of unnecessary work. If you start to apply some 80/20 thinking, you'll quickly find many of those leveraged activities in your own work.

**Progress**   No matter where you reside on any Pareto distribution, you can increase your output exponentially by "moving to the left" using your success habit and the power of focus. As long as the optimum hasn't been reached, there's always room for progress, for reaching more with less—even if you're already a highly developed individual, company, or economy.

The activities that can move you up the Pareto curve are not always obvious, but they are never random. Many people give up searching for the success metrics in their fields because they argue that the probabilistic nature of the outcomes makes it completely random. What a wrong conclusion! To become a master coder, writing less code per day won't get you there just as practicing less chess every day cannot lead you to becoming a professional chess player. Other factors will come into play, but that doesn't make success a game of chance. By focusing on the success metrics in your industry, you will manipulate the probabilities in your favor. As an 80/20 thinker, you are the house—and the house *mostly* wins.

## 80/20 Practice Tips

Let's finish this chapter with nine tips to leverage the power of the Pareto principle.

**Figure out your success metrics.**

Define your industry first. Identify what the most successful professionals in your industry are doing exceptionally well and which tasks you can do every day to push you closer toward the top 20 percent. If you're a coder, your success metric may be the number of lines of code written. If you're an author, your success metric may be the number of words written toward the next book. Create a spreadsheet and track your success metric every day. Make it a game to stick to it and surpass yourself. Set a minimum threshold, and don't end the day until you've accomplished the minimal threshold each day. Better yet, don't start the day until you have!

**Figure out your big goals in life.**

Write them down. Without clearly defined big goals (think: 10-year goals), you won't stick to one thing for a sufficiently long time. You have seen that a critical strategy for moving up the Pareto curve is to stay in the game longer while participating in fewer games.

**Look for ways to achieve the same things with fewer resources.**

How can you accomplish 80 percent of the result in 20 percent of the time? Can you remove the remaining activities that take 80 percent of the time but lead only to 20 percent of the results? If not, can you outsource them? Fiverr and Upwork are cheap ways to find talent, and it pays to leverage the skills of other people.

**Reflect on your own successes.**

What did you do that led to great results? How can you do more of those things?

**Reflect on your own failures.**

How can you do less of the things that are responsible for the failure?

**Read more books in your industry.**

By reading more books, you simulate practical experience without the massive time and energy investment of actually experiencing it. You learn from the mistakes of others. You learn about new ways of doing things. You acquire more skills in your field. A highly educated expert coder can solve a problem 10–100 times quicker than a beginner can. Reading books in your field is likely to be one of the success metrics in your field that will catapult you to success.

**Spend much of your time improving and tweaking existing products.**

Do this rather than inventing new products. Again, this comes from the Pareto distribution. If you have one product in your business, you can invest all your energy pushing this one product up the Pareto curve, generating exponentially increasing results for you and your company. But if you create new products all the time without improving and optimizing the old ones, you'll always have subaverage products. Never forget: the big results are found on the left of the Pareto distribution.

**Smile.**

It's surprising how simple some consequences are. If you're a positive person, many things will be easier. More people will collaborate with you. You'll experience more positivity, happiness, and support. Smiling is a highly leveraged activity with massive impact and little cost.

**Don't do things that reduce value.**

These are things like smoking, eating unhealthily, sleeping little, drinking alcohol, and watching too much Netflix. Avoiding things that drag you down is one of your biggest leverage points. If you skip doing things that harm you, you'll become healthier, happier, and more successful. And you'll have more time and money to enjoy the good things in life: relationships, nature, and positive experiences.

In the next chapter, you'll learn a key concept that helps you focus on the vital few features of your software: you'll learn how to build a minimum viable product.

## Resources

Let's have a look at the sources used in this chapter—feel free to explore them further to find more applications of the Pareto principle!

Panagiotis Louridas, Diomidis Spinellis, and Vasileios Vlachos, "Power Laws in Software," *ACM Transactions on Software Engineering and Methodology* 18, no. 1 (September 2008), *https://doi.org/10.1145/1391984.1391986/.*

Scientific evidence that contributions to open source projects are Pareto distributed:

Mathieu Goeminne and Tom Mens, "Evidence for the Pareto Principle in Open Source Software Activity," Conference: CSMR 2011 Workshop on Software Quality and Maintainability (SQM), January 2011, *https://www.researchgate.net/publication/228728263_Evidence_for_the_Pareto_principle_in_Open_Source_Software_Activity/*.

Source for the commit distribution in the GitHub repository TensorFlow:

*https://github.com/tensorflow/tensorflow/graphs/contributors/*.

My blog article on the income distribution of freelance developers:

Christian Mayer, "What's the Hourly Rate of a Python Freelancer?" *Finxter* (blog), *https://blog.finxter.com/whats-the-hourly-rate-of-a-python-freelancer/*.

Scientific evidence that open markets adhere to the Pareto principles:

William J. Reed, "The Pareto Law of Incomes—an Explanation and an Extension," *Physica A: Statistical Mechanics and its Applications* 319 (March 2003), *https://doi.org/10.1016/S0378-4371(02)01507-8/*.

A paper that shows the fractal nature of income distributions:

Fatimah Abdul Razak and Faridatulazna Ahmad Shahabuddin, "Malaysian Household Income Distribution: A Fractal Point of View," *Sains Malaysianna* 47, no. 9 (2018), *http://dx.doi.org/10.17576/jsm-2018-4709-29/*.

Information about how you can build your side income as a freelance developer with Python:

Christian Mayer, "How to Build Your High-Income Skill Python." Video, *https://blog.finxter.com/webinar-freelancer/*.

Python Freelancer resource page, *Finxter* (blog), *https://blog.finxter.com/python-freelancing/*.

A deeper dive into the power of 80/20 thinking:

Richard Koch, *The 80/20 Principle: The Secret to Achieving More with Less*, London: Nicholas Brealey, 1997.

Ten percent of the people earn almost 50 percent of the income in the United States:

Facundo Alvaredo, Lucas Chancel, Thomas Piketty, Emmanuel Saez, and Gabriel Zucman, *World Inequality Report 2018*, World Inequality Lab, *https://wir2018.wid.world/files/download/wir2018-summary-english.pdf*.

Less than 25 percent of the people in North America rate their happiness a 9 or 10 on a 0–10 scale where "the worst possible life" is a 0 and "the best possible life" is a 10:

> John Helliwell, Richard Layard, and Jeffrey Sachs, eds., *World Happiness Report 2016, Update* (Vol. 1). New York: Sustainable Development Solutions Network, *https://worldhappiness.report/ed/2016/*.

Twenty percent of book authors may achieve 97 percent of book sales:

> Xindi Wang, Burcu Yucesoy, Onur Varol, Tina Eliassi-Rad, and Albert-László Barabási, "Success in Books: Predicting Book Sales Before Publication," *EPJ Data Sci.* 8, no. 31 (October 2019), *https://doi.org/10.1140/epjds/s13688-019-0208-6/*.

> Jordi Prats, "Harry Potter and Pareto's Fat Tail," *Significance* (August 10, 2011), *https://www.significancemagazine.com/14-the-statistics-dictionary/105-harry-potter-and-pareto-s-fat-tail/*.

Of scientists, 5.2 percent account for 38 percent of journal articles:

> Javier Ruiz-Castillo and Rodrigo Costas, "Individual and Field Citation Distributions in 29 Broad Scientific Fields," *Journal of Informetrics* 12, no. 3 (August 2018), *https://doi.org/10.1016/j.joi.2018.07.002/*.

# 3

## BUILD A MINIMUM VIABLE PRODUCT

This chapter covers a well-known but still undervalued idea popularized in Eric Ries's book *The Lean Startup* (Crown Business, 2011). The idea is to build a *minimum viable product (MVP)*, which is a version of your product stripped of all except the most necessary features, in order to test and validate your hypotheses quickly without losing a lot of time in implementing features your users may not end up using. In particular, you'll learn how to radically reduce complexity in the software development cycle by focusing on features you know your users want, because they've confirmed as much from your MVP.

In this chapter, we'll introduce MVPs by looking at the pitfalls of developing software without using MVPs. We'll then elaborate on the concept in more detail and provide you with a number of practical tips on how to use MVPs in your own projects to accelerate progress.

## A Problem Scenario

The idea behind building an MVP is to combat problems that arise when you program in stealth mode (see Figure 3-1). *Stealth mode* is when you work on a project to completion without seeking any feedback from potential users. Say you come up with a wonderful idea for a program that will change the world: a machine learning–enhanced search engine specifically for searching for code. You start coding enthusiastically on your idea a few nights in a row.

The stealth mode of programming

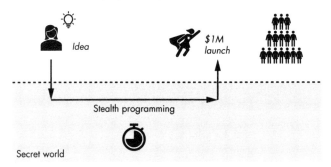

*Figure 3-1: The stealth mode of programming consists of keeping the app secret until the final polished version can be released in the hope of immediate success. In most cases, this is a fallacy.*

However, in practice, coding an app in one go leads to immediate success very, very, very rarely. Here's a more likely outcome of following the stealth mode of programming:

You quickly develop the prototype, but when you try your search engine, you find that many search terms in the recommended results are not relevant. When you search for Quicksort, you obtain a MergeSort code snippet with a comment # This is not Quicksort. That doesn't seem right. So, you keep tweaking the models, but each time you improve the results for one keyword, you create new problems for other search results. You're never quite happy with the result, and you don't feel like you can present your crappy code search engine to the world for three reasons: nobody will find it useful; the first users will create negative publicity around your website because it won't feel professional and polished; and you worry that if competitors see your poorly implemented concept, they'll steal it and implement it in a better way. These depressing thoughts cause you to lose faith and motivation, and your progress on the app drops to zero.

Figure 3-2 depicts what can and will go wrong in the stealth mode of programming.

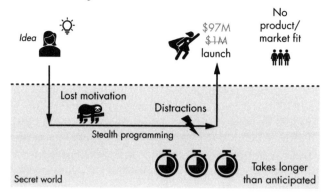

*What went wrong?*

*Figure 3-2: Common pitfalls in the stealth mode of programming*

Here I'll discuss the six most common pitfalls of working in stealth mode.

## Loss of Motivation

In stealth mode, you're alone with your idea, and doubts will pop up regularly. You resist the doubts initially, while your initial enthusiasm for the project is big enough, but the longer you work on your project, the bigger your doubts grow. Maybe you come across a similar tool already in existence, or you start to believe that it cannot be done. Loss of motivation can kill your project entirely.

On the other hand, if you release an early version of the tool, encouraging words from an early adopter could keep you motivated enough to persevere, and feedback from users might inspire you to improve the tool or overcome problems. You have external motivation.

## Distraction

When you work alone in stealth mode, daily distractions are difficult to ignore. You work in your day job, you spend time with family and friends, other ideas pop into your mind. These days, your attention is a rare good sought by many devices and services. The longer you are in stealth mode, the higher the likelihood of getting distracted before ever finishing your polished app.

An MVP can combat this by reducing the time from idea to market response, creating an environment of more immediate feedback that helps refocus your attention. And who knows—maybe you'll find some eager early users of your MVP that can help propel the application development.

## Running Over Time

Another powerful enemy of project completion is faulty planning. Say you estimate that your product will take 60 hours to complete, so you initially plan to work on it for 2 hours every day for a month. However, loss of motivation and distractions cause you to average only 1 hour every day. Further delays are caused by research you have to commit to, external distractions, and unexpected events and bugs that you must work around. An infinite number of factors will increase your anticipated project duration, and few will reduce it. By the end of the first month, you're nowhere near where you thought you'd be, feeding back into the loss-of-motivation loop.

An MVP is stripped of all unnecessary features. Thus, your planning mistakes will be fewer, and your progress will be more predictable. Having fewer features means fewer things will go wrong. Furthermore, the more predictable your project, the more you or the people invested in your project will believe in its success. Investors and stakeholders love predictability!

## Lack of Response

Say you overcome your low motivation and complete the product. You finally launch it, and nothing happens. Only a handful of users even check it out, and they're not enthusiastic about it. The most likely outcome of any software project is silence—an absence of positive or negative feedback. A common reason is that your product doesn't deliver the specific value the users demand. It's almost impossible to find the so-called *product-market fit* in your first shot. If you don't get any feedback from the real world during development, you start to drift away from reality, working on features nobody will use.

Your MVP will help you find product-market fit much quicker because, as you'll see later in this chapter, an MVP-based approach develops the project to directly address the most pressing customer needs, increasing your chances of customer engagement and therefore response to early product versions.

## Wrong Assumptions

The main cause of failure in stealth mode is your own assumptions. You start a project with a bunch of assumptions, such as who the users will be, what they do for a living, what problems they face, or how often they will use your product. These assumptions are often wrong, and without external testing, you carry on blindly creating products your actual audience does not want. Once you get no feedback or negative feedback, it corrodes any motivation.

When I was creating my app for learning Python by solving rated code puzzles, I assumed that most users would be computer science students because I was one (reality: most users are not computer scientists). I assumed that users would come when I released the app (reality: nobody came initially). I assumed that many users would share their successes via their social media accounts (reality: only a tiny minority of users shared their coding ranks). I assumed that users would submit their own code puzzles (reality: from hundreds of thousands of users, only a handful submitted code puzzles). I assumed that users wanted a fancy design with colors and images (reality: a simple geeky design led to improved usage behavior—see Chapter 8 on simple designs). All those assumptions led to concrete implementation decisions that cost me tens, if not hundreds, of hours implementing many features my audience did not want. If I'd known better, I would have tested these assumptions in an MVP, responded to user feedback, saved myself time and energy, and reduced the likelihood of jeopardizing the project's success.

## Unnecessary Complexity

There's another problem with the stealth mode of programming: *unnecessary complexity*. Say you implement a software product that includes four features (see Figure 3-3). You've been lucky—the market accepted it. You've spent considerable time implementing those four features, and you take the positive feedback as a reinforcement for all four features. All future releases of the software product will contain those four features—in addition to the features you'll add in the future.

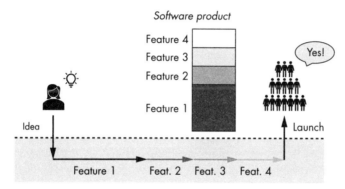

Figure 3-3: A valuable software product consisting of four features

However, by releasing the package of four features at once rather than one or two features at a time, you don't know whether the market would've accepted, or even preferred, any subset of features (see Figure 3-4).

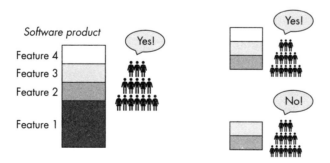

Figure 3-4: Which subsets of features would have been accepted by the market?

Feature 1 may be completely irrelevant, even though it took you the most time to implement. At the same time, Feature 4 may be a highly valuable feature that the market demands. There are $2^n$ different combinations of software product packages out of $n$ features. If you release them as feature bundles, how can you possibly know which is valuable and which is a waste of time?

The costs of implementing the wrong features are already high, and releasing bundles of wrong features incurs the cumulative costs of maintaining unnecessary features:

- Longer, feature-heavy projects require more time to "load" the whole project in your mind.

- Each feature risks introducing new bugs.

- Each line of code adds time cost to opening, loading, and compiling the project.

- Implementing feature $n$ requires you to check all previous features $1, 2, \ldots, n-1$ to ensure that feature $n$ doesn't interfere with their functionality.

- Every new feature requires new unit tests that must compile and run before you can release the next version of the code.

- Every added feature makes the codebase more complicated for a coder to understand, increasing learning time for new coders joining the project.

This is not an exhaustive list, but you get the point. If each feature increases your future implementation costs by $x$ percent, maintaining unnecessary features can result in orders of magnitude difference in coding productivity. You cannot afford to systematically keep unnecessary features in your code projects!

So, you may ask: If the stealth mode of programming is unlikely to succeed, what's the solution?

## Building a Minimum Viable Product

The solution is simple: build a series of MVPs. Formulate an explicit hypothesis—such as *users enjoy solving Python puzzles*—and create a product that validates only this hypothesis. Remove all features that don't help you validate this hypothesis. Build an MVP based on that feature. By implementing just a single feature per release, you more thoroughly understand what features the marketplace accepts and which hypotheses are true. But at all costs, avoid complexity. After all, if users don't enjoy solving Python puzzles, why even proceed with implementing the Finxter.com website? Once you've tested your MVP on the real-world market and analyzed whether it works, you can build a second MVP that adds the next most important feature. The term to describe this strategy of searching for the right product via a series of MVPs is called *rapid prototyping*. Each prototype builds on what you learn from the previous launches, and each is designed to bring you maximal learning in minimal time and with minimum effort. You *release early and often* in order to find *product-market fit*, which entails nailing the product needs and desires of your target market (even if this target market is very small in the beginning).

Let's look at an example using the code search engine. You first formulate a hypothesis to test: coders need a way to search for code. Think about what form the first MVP might take for your code search engine app. A shell-based API? A backend server that performs a database lookup on all open source GitHub projects for exact word matches? The first MVP must validate the main hypotheses. Thus, you decide the simplest way to validate this hypothesis and gain some insight into possible queries is to build a user interface without any sophisticated backend functionality that automatically retrieves results for the query. You set up a website with an input field and drive some traffic to it by sharing your idea in coding groups and on social media and by spending a small amount on ads. The app interface is simple: users enter the code they want to search for and hit a search button. You don't bother optimizing the search results too much; this is not the point of your first MVP. Instead, you decide to simply relay Google's search results after a quick postprocessing. The point is to collect the first, say, 100 search queries to find some common user behavior patterns before you even start developing the search engine!

You analyze the data and find that 90 percent of the search queries are related to error messages; coders are simply copying and pasting their coding errors into the search field. Furthermore, you find that 60 out of the 90 queries concern JavaScript. You conclude that the initial hypothesis is validated: coders do indeed search for code. However, you learn the valuable information that most coders search for errors than for, say, functions. Based on your analysis, you decide to narrow your second MVP from a general-purpose code search engine to an *error* search engine. This way, you can tailor your product to the actual user needs and get more engaged feedback from a subsection of coders in order to learn quickly and integrate your learning in a useful product. You can always scale to other languages and query types over time as you gain more and more traction and market insights. Without your first MVP, you may have spent months working on features almost nobody uses, like regular expression functionality to find arbitrary patterns in the code, at the cost of features everybody uses like error message searches.

Figure 3-5 sketches this gold standard of software development and product creation. First, you find product-market fit through iteratively launching MVPs until users love your product. The chained launches of MVPs build interest over time and allow you to incorporate user feedback to gradually improve the core idea of your software. As soon as you've reached product-market fit, you add new features—one at a time. Only if a feature can prove that it improves key user metrics does it remain in the product.

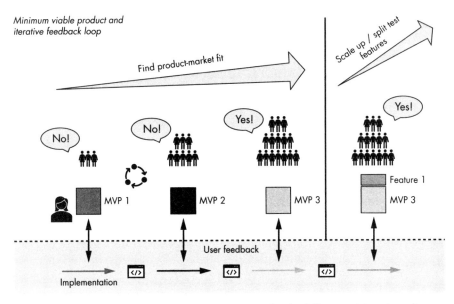

*Figure 3-5: Two phases of software development involve the following: (1) Find product-market fit through iterative MVP creation and build interest over time. (2) Scale up by adding and validating new features through carefully designed split tests.*

Using Finxter.com as an example, if I had followed the MVP rule from the start, I would probably have created a simple Instagram account that shared code puzzles and checked if users enjoyed solving them. Instead of spending a year writing the app without validation, I could've spent a few weeks or even months sharing puzzles on a social network. Then, I could've taken lessons learned from interacting with the community to build a second MVP with slightly more functionality, such as a dedicated website that hosts the coding puzzles and their correct solutions. This method would have allowed me to build the app in a fraction of the time and with a fraction of the unnecessary features. The lesson of building an MVP stripped from all unnecessary features is one I've learned the hard way.

In *The Lean Startup*, Eric Ries discusses how the billion-dollar company Dropbox famously adopted the MVP approach. Instead of spending time and effort on an untested idea to implement the complicated Dropbox functionality of synchronizing folder structures into the cloud—which requires a tight integration in different operating systems and a thorough implementation of burdensome distributed systems concepts such as replica synchronization—the founders validated the idea with a simple product video, even though the product featured in the video didn't exist yet. Countless iterations followed the validated Dropbox MVP to add more helpful features to the core project that simplify the lives of their users. Since then, the concept has been tested by thousands of successful companies in the software industry (and beyond).

If the market signals that users love and value your product idea, you've achieved product-market fit with just a simple, well-crafted MVP. From there, you can iteratively build and refine your MVPs.

When you use an MVP-based approach for software development, adding one feature at a time, it's important to be able to identify which feature to keep and which to reject. The final step of the MVP software creation process is *split testing*: rather than release the iterations with new features to your entire user base, you launch the new product to a fraction of your users and observe the implicit and explicit response. Only if you like what you see—for example, the average time spent on your website increases—do you keep the feature. Otherwise, you reject it and stay with the previous iteration without the feature. This means you must sacrifice the time and energy you spent developing the feature, but it does allow you to keep your product as simple as possible, allowing you to remain agile, flexible, and efficient. By using split tests, you engage in data-driven software development.

## Four Pillars of Building a Minimum Viable Product

When building your first software based on MVP thinking, consider these four pillars:

**Functionality** The product provides a clearly formulated function to the user, and it does it well. The function doesn't have to be provided with great economic efficiency. Your MVP for a chat bot might actually just be you chatting with the user yourself; this clearly could not scale, but you're demonstrating the functionality of high-quality chatting—even if you haven't figured out how to provide this functionality in an economically feasible way yet.

**Design** The product is well designed and focused, and its design supports the value that your product offers to your target niche. One common mistake in MVP generation is that you create an interface that doesn't accurately reflect your single-function MVP website. The design can be straightforward, but it must support the value proposition. Think Google Search—they certainly didn't spend lots of effort on design when releasing their first version of the search engine, but the design was well suited for the product they offered: distraction-free search.

**Reliability** Just because your product is minimal doesn't mean it can be unreliable. Make sure to write test cases and test all functions in your code rigorously. Otherwise, your learnings from the MVP will be corrupted by the negative user feedback based on its unreliability, and not feedback on the features directly. Remember: you want to maximize learning with minimal effort.

**Usability** The MVP must be easy to use. The functionality is clearly articulated, and the design supports it. Users don't need to spend a lot of time figuring out what to do or which buttons to click. The MVP is responsive and fast enough to allow fluent interactions. This is often simpler to achieve with a focused, minimalistic product: it is obvious how you should use a page with one button and one input field. Again, the Google search engine's initial prototype is a prime example, and it was so usable that it lasted for more than two decades.

Many people misunderstand this characteristic of MVPs: they wrongly assume that, because it's an extremely minimalist version of a product, an MVP must provide little value, bad usability, and a lazy design. However, the minimalist knows that the concision of an MPV actually comes from a rigorous focus on one core functionality rather than from lazy product creation. For Dropbox, creating an effective video showcasing intention was easier than implementing the service itself. The MVP was a high-quality product with great functionality, design, reliability, and usability.

## Advantages of the Minimum Viable Product

The advantages of MVP-driven software design are manifold.

- You can test your hypotheses as cheaply as possible.
- You can often avoid actually writing the code until you know it's necessary, and then when you do write code, you minimize the amount of work before gathering real-world feedback.
- You spend much less time writing code and finding bugs—and you'll know the time you do spend is highly valuable for your users.
- Any new feature you ship to users provides instant feedback, and the continuous progress keeps you and your team motivated to crank out feature after feature. This dramatically minimizes the risks you're exposed to in the stealth mode of programming.
- You reduce the maintenance costs in the future because the MVP approach reduces the complexity of your codebase by a long shot—and all future features will be easier and less error prone.
- You'll make faster progress, and implementation will be easier throughout the life of your software—which keeps you in a motivated state and on the road to success.
- You'll ship products faster, earn money from your software faster, and build your brand more predictably and reliably.

## Stealth vs. Minimum Viable Product Approach

A common counterargument against rapid prototyping and *for* the stealth mode of programming is that stealth programming protects your ideas. People assume their idea is special and unique enough that if they release it in the raw form, as an MVP, it will get stolen by larger and more powerful companies that can implement it more quickly. Frankly, this is a fallacy. Ideas are cheap; execution is king. Any given idea is unlikely to be unique, and there's a strong chance your idea has already been thought of by some other person. Rather than reducing competition, the stealth mode of programming may even encourage others to work on the same idea, because like you, they assume that nobody else has already thought of it. For an idea to succeed, it takes a person to push it into reality. If you fast-forward a few years, the person that succeeded will be the one who took quick and decisive action, released early and often, incorporated feedback from real users, and gradually improved their software by building on the momentum of previous releases. Keeping the idea secret would simply restrict its growth potential.

## Conclusion

Envision your end product and think about the needs of your users before you write any code. Work on your MVP and make it valuable, well designed, responsive, and usable. Remove all features but those that are absolutely necessary to achieve the goal. Focus on one thing at a time. Then, release MVPs quickly and often—improve them over time by gradually testing and adding more features. Less is more! Spend more time thinking about the next feature to implement than you spend actually implementing each feature. Every feature incurs not only direct but also indirect implementation costs for all features to come in the future. Use split testing to test the response to two product variants at a time and quickly discard features that don't lead to an improvement in your key user metrics, such as retention, time on page, or activity. This leads to a more holistic approach to your business—acknowledging that software development is only one step in the whole product creation and value delivery process.

In the next chapter, you'll learn why and how to write clean and simple code, but remember: not writing unnecessary code is the surest path to clean and simple code!

# 4

## WRITE CLEAN AND SIMPLE CODE

*Clean code* is code that's easy to read, understand, and change. It is minimal and concise, as long as those attributes do not interfere with readability. While writing clean code is more an art than a science, the software engineering industry has agreed on multiple principles that, if followed, will help you write *cleaner* code. In this chapter, you'll learn 17 principles for how to write clean code that will significantly improve your productivity and combat the problem of complexity.

You may wonder about the difference between *clean* and *simple* code. These two concepts are closely interrelated because clean code tends to be simple and simple code tends to be clean. But it's possible to encounter complex code that is still clean. Simplicity concerns the avoidance of complexity. Clean code goes one step further and also concerns itself with managing unavoidable complexity—for instance, through the effective use of comments and standards.

## Why Write Clean Code?

In the previous chapters, you learned that complexity is the number one public enemy for any code project. You've learned that simplicity increases your productivity, your motivation, and the maintainability of your codebase. In this chapter, we'll carry this concept a step further and show you how to write clean code.

Clean code is easier to understand for both your future self and your fellow coders, since people are more likely to add to clean code and the potential for collaboration will increase. Consequently, clean code can significantly reduce a project's costs. As Robert C. Martin points out in his book *Clean Code* (Prentice Hall, 2008), coders spend the vast majority of their time reading old code in order to write new code. If the old code is easy to read, this will speed the process considerably.

> Indeed, the ratio of time spent reading versus writing is well over 10 to 1. We are constantly reading old code as part of the effort to write new code. [Therefore,] making it easy to read makes it easier to write.

If we take this ratio literally, this relationship is visualized in Figure 4-1. The x-axis corresponds to the number of lines written in a given code project. The y-axis corresponds to the time to write one additional line of code. In general, the more code you've already written in one project, the more time it takes to write an additional line of code. This is true for both clean and dirty code.

Say you've written $n$ lines of code, and you add the $n + 1$st line of code. Adding this line may potentially affect all previously written lines. It may, for example, have a small performance penalty, which impacts the overall project. It may use a variable defined somewhere else. It may introduce a bug (with probability $c$), and to find that bug, you must search the whole project. That means your expected time—and therefore, costs—per line of code is $c * T(n)$ for a steadily increasing time function $T$ with increasing input $n$. Adding a line may also force you to write additional lines of code to ensure backward compatibility.

Lengthier code may introduce many other complications, but you get the point: the more code you've written, the more the additional complexity will slow your progress.

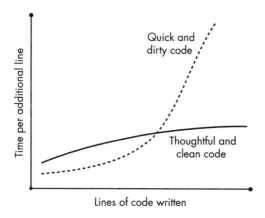

Figure 4-1: Clean code improves the scalability and maintainability of your codebase.

Figure 4-1 also shows the difference between writing dirty and clean code. Dirty code is less time-consuming in the short term and for small code projects—if there were no benefits to writing dirty code, nobody would do it! If you cram all your functionality into a 100-line code script, you don't need to invest a lot of time thinking about and restructuring your project. Problems begin to arise only as you add more code: as your monolithic code file grows from 100 to 1,000 lines, it'll be less efficient than code developed using a more thoughtful approach in which you structure the code logically in different modules, classes, or files.

As a rule of thumb: always write thoughtful and clean code. The additional costs for rethinking, refactoring, and restructuring will pay back many times over for any non-trivial project. The stakes can sometimes be quite high: in 1962 the National Aeronautics and Space Administration (NASA) attempted to send a spacecraft to Venus, but a tiny bug—the omission of a hyphen in the source code—caused the engineers to issue a self-destruct command, which resulted in the loss of a rocket worth more than $18 million at the time. If the code had been cleaner, the engineers may have caught the error before the launch.

Whether or not you're doing rocket science, the philosophy of carefully crafting your programming will carry you further in life. Simple code also facilitates scaling your project to more programmers and more features because fewer coders will be scared off by the project's complexity.

So, let's learn how to write clean and simple code, shall we?

## Writing Clean Code: The Principles

I learned to write clean code the hard way when I was developing a distributed graph-processing system from scratch as part of my doctoral research. If you've ever written a distributed application—where two processes residing on different computers interact with each other via messages—you know that the complexity can quickly become overwhelming. My code grew to thousands of lines, and bugs popped up frequently. I didn't make any progress for weeks at a time; it was very frustrating. The concepts were convincing in theory, but somehow they didn't work in my implementation.

Finally, after a month or so working full-time on the codebase without seeing any encouraging progress, I decided to simplify the codebase radically. Among other changes, I started to use libraries instead of coding functionality myself. I removed code blocks that I had commented out for a possible later use. I renamed variables and functions. I structured the code in logical units and created new classes instead of cramming everything into a "God" class. After a week or so, not only was my code more readable and understandable for other researchers, it was also more efficient and less buggy. My frustration morphed into enthusiasm—clean code had rescued my research project!

Improving your codebase and reducing complexity is called *refactoring*, and it must be a scheduled and crucial element of your software development process if you want to write clean and simple code. Writing clean code is mainly about keeping two things in mind: knowing the best ways to build your code from the ground up and going back to make revisions periodically. I'll cover some important techniques for keeping your code clean in the following 17 principles. While each principle covers a unique strategy to write cleaner code, some of the principles overlap, but I felt like combining the overlapping principles would reduce clarity and actionability. With this out of the way, let's get started with the first one!

## Principle 1: Think About the Big Picture

If you work on a non-trivial project, you'll likely end up with multiple files, modules, and libraries working together within the overall application. Your *software architecture* defines how your software elements interact. Good architectural decisions can initiate huge leaps of improvement in performance, maintainability, and usability. To build a good architecture, you'll need to take a step back and think about the big picture. Decide on features that are needed in the first place. In Chapter 3 about building an MVP, you learned how to focus your project on the necessary features. If you do this, you save yourself a lot of work and the code will be a lot more clean per design. At this point, we assume you've already created your first application with multiple modules, files, and classes. How can you apply big-picture thinking to impose some order on the mess? Considering the following questions can give you some ideas on how to best make your code cleaner:

- Do you need all the separate files and modules, or can you consolidate some of them and reduce the interdependency of your code?
- Can you divide a large and complicated file into two simpler ones? Note that there's usually a sweet spot between two extremes: a large, monolithic code block that is completely unreadable or a myriad of small code blocks that are impossible to mentally keep track of. Neither

is desirable, and most stages in between are better options. Think of it as an inverted U curve where the maximum represents the sweet spot between a few large code blocks and many small code blocks.

- Can you generalize code and turn it into a library to simplify the main application?
- Can you use existing libraries to get rid of many lines of code?
- Can you use caching to avoid recomputing the same result over and over again?
- Can you use more straightforward and suitable algorithms that accomplish the same things as your current algorithms?
- Can you remove premature optimizations that don't improve the overall performance?
- Can you use another programming language that would be more suitable for the problem at hand?

Big-picture thinking is a time-efficient way to drastically reduce the complexity of your application as a whole. Sometimes it's hard to implement those changes at later various stages of the process or because of collaborations that might interfere. In particular, this kind of high-level thinking can be difficult for applications with millions of lines of code, like the Windows operating system. However, you simply cannot afford to ignore these questions entirely because all the small tweaks combined cannot mitigate the adverse effects of wrong or lazy design choices. If you're working in a small startup or just for yourself, you can usually make bold architectural decisions, such as changing the algorithm, swiftly. If you're working in a big organization, you might not have as much flexibility. The bigger the application, the more likely you are to find easy fixes and low-hanging fruit.

## Principle 2: Stand on the Shoulders of Giants

Reinventing the wheel is rarely valuable. Programming is a decades-old industry. The best coders in the world have provided us with a great legacy: a database of millions of fine-tuned and well-tested algorithms and code functions. Accessing the collective wisdom of millions of programmers is as simple as using a one-line import statement. There's no reason not to use this superpower in your own projects.

Using library code is likely to improve the efficiency of your code. Functions that have been used by thousands of coders tend to be much more optimized than your own. Furthermore, library calls are easier to understand and take less space in your code project than code you've written in yourself. For example, suppose you need a clustering algorithm to visualize clusters of customers. You can *stand on the shoulders of giants* by importing a well-tested clustering algorithm from an external library and passing your data into it. This is far more time-efficient than using your own code—it will implement the same functionality with fewer bugs, less space, and more performant code. Libraries are among the primary tools that master coders use to increase their productivity thousandfold.

As an example of some library code that can save you time, here's the two-liner that imports the KMeans module from the scikit-learn Python library to find two cluster centers on a given dataset stored in variable X:

```
from sklearn.cluster import KMeans
kmeans = KMeans(n_clusters=2, random_state=0).fit(X)
```

Implementing the KMeans algorithm on your own instead would take you several hours and likely more than 50 lines of code, cluttering your codebase so that all future code would become harder to implement.

## Principle 3: Code for People, Not Machines

You may think that the primary purpose of a piece of source code is to define what machines should do and how they should do it. Not so. The single purpose of a programming language such as Python is to help humans write code. Compilers do the heavy lifting and translate your high-level code to low-level code that is understandable by your machine. Yes, your code will eventually be run by a machine. But code is still written mainly by humans, and in today's software development process, the code likely must pass many levels of human judgment before it is deployed. First and foremost, you're writing code for people, not machines.

Always assume that others will read your source code. Imagine you moved to a new project and someone else had to take your place at the codebase. There are many ways to make their job easier and minimize frustration. First of all, use meaningful variable names so that readers can easily follow what a given line of code is intended to accomplish. Listing 4-1 shows an example of poorly chosen variable names.

```
xxx = 10000
yyy = 0.1
zzz = 10

for iii in range(zzz):
    print(xxx * (1 + yyy)**iii)
```

Listing 4-1: Code that uses poorly chosen variable names

It's difficult to guess what this code computes. Listing 4-2, on the other hand, is a semantically equivalent code that uses meaningful variable names.

```
investments = 10000
yearly_return = 0.1
years = 10

for year in range(years):
    print(investments * (1 + yearly_return)**year)
```

Listing 4-2: Code that uses meaningful variable names

It's much easier to understand what's happening here: the variable names indicate how to calculate the value of an initial investment of 10,000 compounded over 10 years, assuming an annual return of 10 percent.

While we won't go into every way to implement this principle here (though later principles will cover some approaches in more detail), it also manifests in other aspects that might clarify intent, such as indentation, whitespace, comments, and line lengths, among others. Clean code radically optimizes for human readability. As Martin Fowler, an international expert on software engineering and author of the popular book *Refactoring*, argues, "Any fool can write code that a computer can understand. Good programmers write code that humans can understand" (Addison-Wesley, 1999).

### Principle 4: Use the Right Names

Relatedly, experienced coders have often agreed on a set of specific naming conventions for functions, function arguments, objects, methods, and variables, both implicit and explicit. Everybody benefits from adhering to these conventions: code becomes more readable, easier to understand, and less cluttered. If you violate these conventions, readers of your code are likely to assume that it was written by an inexperienced programmer and may not take your code seriously.

These conventions may differ from language to language. For example, by convention Java uses `camelCaseNaming` for naming variables, while Python uses `underscore_naming` for variables and functions. If you start using camel case in Python, it may confuse the reader. You don't want your untraditional naming conventions to distract those reading your code. You want them to focus on what your code does, not on your coding style. As outlined by the *principle of least surprise*, there's no value in surprising other coders by choosing unconventional variable names.

So, let's dive into a list of naming rules you can consider when writing source code.

**Choose descriptive names**  Say you create a function to convert currencies from United States dollars (USD) to euros (EUR) in Python. Call it `usd_to_eur(amount)` rather than `f(x)`.

**Choose unambiguous names**  You may think that `dollar_to_euro` `(amount)` would be a good name for a currency conversion function. While it is better than `f(x)`, it's worse than `usd_to_eur(amount)` because it introduces an unnecessary degree of ambiguity. Do you mean United States, Canadian, or Australian dollars? If you're in the United States, the answer may be obvious to you, but an Australian coder may not know that the code is written in the United States and may assume a different output. Minimize these confusions!

**Use pronounceable names**  Most coders subconsciously read code by pronouncing it in their minds. If a variable name is unpronounceable, the problem of deciphering it takes attention and costs precious mental space. For example, the variable name `cstmr_lst` may be descriptive and unambiguous, but it's not pronounceable. Choosing the variable name `customer_list` is well worth the additional space in your code.

**Use named constants, not magic numbers**  In your code, you may use the magic number 0.9 multiple times as a factor to convert a sum in USD to a sum in EUR. However, the reader of your code—including your future self—has to think about the purpose of this number. It's not self-explanatory. A far better way of handling the magic number 0.9 is to store it in an all-uppercase variable—used to indicate that it is a constant that doesn't change—such as `CONVERSION_RATE = 0.9` and use it as a factor in your conversion computations. For example, you may then calculate your income in EUR as `income_euro = CONVERSION_RATE * income_usd`.

These are only a few naming rules. Beyond these quick tips, the best way to learn naming conventions is to study the well-crafted code of experts. Googling the relevant conventions (for example, "Python naming conventions") is a good place to start. You might also read programming tutorials, join StackOverflow to query fellow coders, check out the GitHub code of open source projects, and join the Finxter blog community of ambitious coders who help each other grow their programming skills.

## Principle 5: Adhere to Standards and Be Consistent

Every programming language comes with an implicit or explicit set of rules on how to write clean code. If you are an active coder, these standards will always catch up with you eventually. However, you can speed the process by taking the time to study the code standard of the programming language you're learning.

For example, you can access the official Python style guide, PEP 8, at this link: *https://www.python.org/dev/peps/pep-0008/*. As with any style guide, PEP 8 defines the correct code layout and indentation; the method to set line breaks; the maximum number of characters in a line; the correct use of commenting; the formulation of your own function documentation; and the conventions for naming classes, variables, and functions. For instance, Listing 4-3 shows a positive example from PEP 8's guidelines on the correct way to use different stylings and conventions. You use four spaces per indentation level, align function arguments consistently, use single whitespaces when listing comma-separated values in argument lists, and correctly name functions and variables by combining multiple words with the underscore:

```
# Aligned with the opening delimiter.
foo = long_function_name(var_one, var_two,
                         var_three, var_four)

# Add 4 spaces (an extra level of indentation) to distinguish
# arguments from the rest.
def long_function_name(
        var_one, var_two, var_three,
        var_four):
    print(var_one)
```

```
# Hanging indents should add a level.
foo = long_function_name(
    var_one, var_two,
    var_three, var_four)
```

*Listing 4-3: Use of indentation, spacing, and naming in Python according to the PEP 8 standard*

Listing 4-4 shows the wrong way to do it. The arguments are not aligned, multiple words are not properly combined in variable and function names, argument lists are not properly separated by a single empty space, and indentation levels have only two or three empty spaces instead of four:

```
# Arguments on first line forbidden when not using vertical alignment.
foo = longFunctionName(varone,varTwo,
   var3,varxfour)

# Further indentation required as indentation is not distinguishable.
def longfunctionname(
  var1,var2,var3,
  var4):
  print(var_one)
```

*Listing 4-4: Incorrect use of indentation, spacing, and naming in Python*

All readers of your code will expect you to adhere to the accepted standards. Anything else will result in confusion and frustration.

Reading through style guides can be a tedious task, though. As a less boring way to learn conventions and standards, use linters and integrated development environments (IDEs) that tell you where and how you've made mistakes. In a weekend hackathon with my team, we created a tool called Pythonchecker.com that playfully helps you refactor your Python code from messy to super clean. For Python, one of the best projects in this regard is the *black* module for PyCharm. Similar tools exist for all major programming languages. Just search the net for *<Your Language> Linter* to find the best tools for your programming environment.

## Principle 6: Use Comments

As mentioned earlier, when writing code for humans, not machines, you'll need to use comments to help readers understand it. Consider the code without comments in Listing 4-5.

```
import re

text = '''
    Ha! let me see her: out, alas! She's cold:
    Her blood is settled, and her joints are stiff;
    Life and these lips have long been separated:
    Death lies on her like an untimely frost
    Upon the sweetest flower of all the field.
'''
```

```
f_words = re.findall('\\bf\w+\\b', text)
print(f_words)


l_words = re.findall('\\bl\w+\\b', text)
print(l_words)

'''

OUTPUT:
['frost', 'flower', 'field']
['let', 'lips', 'long', 'lies', 'like']

'''
```

*Listing 4-5: Code without comments*

Listing 4-5 analyzes a short text snippet from Shakespeare's *Romeo and Juliet* using regular expressions. If you're not familiar with regular expressions, you'll probably struggle to understand what the code does. Even the meaningful variable names don't help much.

Let's see if a few comments can resolve your confusion (see Listing 4-6).

```
import re

text = '''
    Ha! let me see her: out, alas! She's cold:
    Her blood is settled, and her joints are stiff;
    Life and these lips have long been separated:
    Death lies on her like an untimely frost
    Upon the sweetest flower of all the field.
'''

❶ # Find all words starting with character 'f'.
  f_words = re.findall('\\bf\w+\\b', text)
  print(f_words)

❷ # Find all words starting with character 'l'.
  l_words = re.findall('\\bl\w+\\b', text)
  print(l_words)

  '''
  OUTPUT:
  ['frost', 'flower', 'field']
  ['let', 'lips', 'long', 'lies', 'like']
  '''
```

*Listing 4-6: Code with comments*

The two short comments (❶ ❷) illuminate the purpose of the regular expression patterns '\\bf\w+\\b' and '\\bl\w+\\b'. I won't dive deeply into regular expressions here, but the example shows how comments can help you get a rough understanding of other people's code without understanding the syntactic sugar.

You can also use comments to abstract over blocks of code. For example, if you have five code lines that deal with updating customer information in a database, add a short comment before the block to explain this, as in Listing 4-7.

```
❶ # Process next order
order = get_next_order()
user = order.get_user()
database.update_user(user)
database.update_product(order.get_order())

❷ # Ship order & confirm customer
logistics.ship(order, user.get_address())
user.send_confirmation()
```

Listing 4-7: Commented blocks give an overview of the code.

This shows how an online shop completes a customer order in two high-level steps: processing the next order ❶ and shipping the order ❷. The comments help you understand the purpose of the code quickly without needing to decipher each method call.

You can also use comments to warn programmers of potentially undesirable consequences. For example, Listing 4-8 alerts us that calling the function ship_yacht() will actually ship an expensive yacht to a customer.

```
############################################################
# WARNING                                                  #
# EXECUTING THIS FUNCTION WILL SHIP A $1,569,420 YACHT!! #
############################################################
def ship_yacht(customer):
    database.update(customer.get_address())
    logistics.ship_yacht(customer.get_address())
    logistics.send_confirmation(customer)
```

Listing 4-8: Comments as warnings

You can employ comments in many more useful ways; they are not only about applying the standards correctly. Keep the principle *code for humans* at the top of your mind when writing comments, and you will be fine. As you read code from experienced programmers, you'll absorb the unspoken rules effectively and almost automatically over time. Since you're the expert on code you've written, helpful comments give outsiders a glimpse into your thinking. Don't miss out on sharing your insights with other people!

## Principle 7: Avoid Unnecessary Comments

That said, not all comments help readers understand code better. In some cases, comments actually reduce clarity and confuse the readers of a codebase. To write clean code, you should not only use valuable comments but also avoid unnecessary comments.

During my time as a computer science researcher, a skilled student of mine successfully applied for a job at Google. He told me that the Google headhunters had criticized his code style because he added too many unnecessary comments. Evaluating your comments is another way expert coders can ascertain whether you're a beginner, intermediate, or expert coder yourself. Issues in the code, such as breaking style guides, being lazy or sloppy with comments, or writing non-idiomatic code for a given programming language, are called *code smells* that point to potential problems in the code, and expert coders can spot them a mile away.

How do you know which comments to leave out? In most cases, a comment is unnecessary if it is redundant. For example, if you've used meaningful variable names, the code often becomes self-explanatory and doesn't require line-level comments. Let's look at the code snippet with meaningful variable names in Listing 4-9.

```python
investments = 10000
yearly_return = 0.1
years = 10

for year in range(years):
    print(investments * (1 + yearly_return)**year)
```

*Listing 4-9: Code snippet with meaningful variable names*

It's already clear that the code calculates your cumulative investment return for 10 years, assuming a 10 percent yield. For the sake of argument, let's add some unnecessary comments in Listing 4-10.

```python
investments = 10000 # Your investments, change if needed
yearly_return = 0.1 # Annual return (e.g., 0.1 --> 10%)
years = 10 # Number of years to compound

# Go over each year
for year in range(years):
    # Print value of your investment in current year
    print(investments * (1 + yearly_return)**year)
```

*Listing 4-10: Unnecessary comments*

All comments in Listing 4-10 are redundant. Some would have been useful if you'd chosen less meaningful variable names, but explaining a variable named yearly_return with a comment about it representing the yearly return only adds unnecessary clutter.

In general, you should use common sense to decide whether a comment is necessary, but here are some of the main guidelines.

**Don't use inline comments**   These can be avoided entirely by choosing meaningful variable names.

**Don't add obvious comments**   In Listing 4-10, the comment explaining the for loop statement is unnecessary. Every coder knows the for loop, so there is no additional value in adding the comment # Go over each year given the expression for year in range(years).

**Don't comment out old code; remove it**   We programmers often hang on to our beloved code snippets, even after we've (grudgingly) decided to remove them, by simply commenting them out. This kills your code's readability! Always remove unnecessary code—for peace of mind, you can use a version history tool such as Git that saves earlier drafts of your project.

**Use documentation functionality**   Many programming languages such as Python come with built-in documentation functionality that allows you to describe the purpose of each function, method, and class in your code. If each of these has only a single responsibility (as per Principle 10), it's often enough to use the documentation instead of comments to describe what your code does.

## Principle 8: The Principle of Least Surprise

The principle of least surprise states that a component of a system should behave in the way most users expect it to behave. This principle is one of the golden rules when designing effective applications and user experience. For example, if you open the Google search engine, the cursor will place itself in the search input field so that you can start typing your search keyword right away, just as you would expect: no surprises.

Clean code also leverages this design principle. Say you write a currency converter that converts the user's input from USD to Chinese renminbi. You store the user input in a variable. Which variable name is better suited, user_input or var_x? The principle of least surprise answers this question for you!

## Principle 9: Don't Repeat Yourself

*Don't repeat yourself (DRY)* is a widely recognized principle that recommends, intuitively enough, avoiding repetitive code. For example, take the Python code in Listing 4-11, which prints the same string five times to the shell.

```
print('hello world')
print('hello world')
print('hello world')
print('hello world')
print('hello world')
```

Listing 4-11: Printing hello world five times

Code that is much less repetitive is shown in Listing 4-12.

```
for i in range(5):
    print('hello world')
```

Listing 4-12: Reducing the repetition found in Listing 4-11

The code in Listing 4-12 will print hello world five times, just as Listing 4-11 does, but without redundancy.

Functions can also be a useful tool to reduce repetition. Say you need to convert miles into kilometers in multiple instances in your code, as in Listing 4-13.

First, you create a variable `miles` and convert it to kilometers by multiplying it by 1.60934. Second, you convert 20 miles to kilometers by multiplying 20 by 1.60934, and store the result in the variable `distance`.

```
miles = 100
kilometers = miles * 1.60934

distance = 20 * 1.60934

print(kilometers)
print(distance)


'''
OUTPUT:
160.934
32.1868
'''
```

Listing 4-13: Converting miles to kilometers twice

You've used the same multiplication procedure twice by multiplying the miles value by the factor 1.60934 to convert miles to kilometers. DRY suggests that it would be better to write a function `miles_to_km(miles)` once, as in Listing 4-14, rather than performing the same conversion explicitly in the code multiple times.

```
def miles_to_km(miles):
    return miles * 1.60934


miles = 100
kilometers = miles_to_km(miles)

distance = miles_to_km(20)

print(kilometers)
print(distance)

'''
OUTPUT:
160.934
32.1868
'''
```

Listing 4-14: Using a function to convert miles to kilometers

This way, the code is easier to maintain. You could, for example, tweak the function to increase the conversion accuracy, and you would have to make the change in only one place. In Listing 4-13, you'd have to search the code for all instances to make that improvement. Applying the DRY principle also makes the code easier to understand for human readers. There's little doubt about the purpose of the function miles_to_km(20), but you may have to think harder about the purpose of the computation 20 * 1.60934.

Violations of DRY are often abbreviated as WET: *we enjoy typing, write everything twice*, and *waste everyone's time.*

## Principle 10: Single Responsibility Principle

The single responsibility principle means that every function should have one main task. It's better to use many small functions than one big function accomplishing everything at the same time. The encapsulation of functionality reduces the overall code complexity.

As a rule of thumb, every class and every function should have only one responsibility. Robert C. Martin, the inventor of this principle, defines a *responsibility* as a *reason to change*. His gold standard when defining a class and a function, thus, is to focus them on a single responsibility so that only the programmer who needs this single responsibility changed would request a change in the definition—and no other programmer with other responsibilities would even consider to issue a change request for the class when assuming, of course, that the code is correct. For example, a function that's responsible for reading data from a database wouldn't also be responsible for processing the data. Otherwise, the function would have two reasons to change: a change in the database model and a change in the processing requirements. If there are multiple reasons to change, multiple programmers may change the same class simultaneously. Your class has too many responsibilities and has become messy and cluttered.

Let's consider a small Python example that may run on an ebook reader to model and manage a user's reading experience (Listing 4-15).

```
❶ class Book:

  ❷ def __init__(self):
        self.title = "Python One-Liners"
        self.publisher = "NoStarch"
        self.author = "Mayer"
        self.current_page = 0

    def get_title(self):
        return self.title

    def get_author(self):
        return self.author

    def get_publisher(self):
        return self.publisher
```

```
❸ def next_page(self):
        self.current_page += 1
        return self.current_page

❹ def print_page(self):
        print(f"... Page Content {self.current_page} ...")



❺ python_one_liners = Book()

print(python_one_liners.get_publisher())
# NoStarch

python_one_liners.print_page()
# ... Page Content 0 ...

python_one_liners.next_page()
python_one_liners.print_page()
# ... Page Content 1 ...
```

*Listing 4-15: Modeling the Book class while violating the single responsibility principle*

The code in Listing 4-15 defines the class Book ❶ with four attributes: title, author, publisher, and the current page number. You define getter methods for the attributes ❷, along with some minimal functionality to move to the next page ❸, which may be called each time the user presses a button on the reading device. The function, print_page(), is responsible for printing the current page to the reading device ❹. This is only given as a stub and would be more complicated in the real world. Finally, you create a Book instance named python_one_liners ❺, and you access its attributes via a series of method calls and print statements in the last couple of lines. A real ebook reader implementation, for example, would call the methods next_page() and print_page() each time the user requests a new page when reading the book.

While the code looks clean and simple, it violates the single responsibility principle: the class Book is responsible both for modeling data, such as the book content, and for printing the book to the device. Modeling and printing are two different functions but are encapsulated in a single class. You have multiple reasons to change. You may want to change the modeling of the book's data: for example, you could use a database instead of a file-based input/output method. But you may also want to change the representation of the modeled data by, for example, using another book-formatting scheme on other types of screens.

Let's fix this issue in Listing 4-16.

```
❶ class Book:

❷    def __init__(self):
        self.title = "Python One-Liners"
        self.publisher = "NoStarch"
```

```
        self.author = "Mayer"
        self.current_page = 0

    def get_title(self):
        return self.title

    def get_author(self):
        return self.author

    def get_publisher(self):
        return self.publisher

    def get_page(self):
        return self.current_page

    def next_page(self):
        self.current_page += 1


❸ class Printer:

❹   def print_page(self, book):
        print(f"... Page Content {book.get_page()} ...")



python_one_liners = Book()
printer = Printer()

printer.print_page(python_one_liners)
# ... Page Content 0 ...

python_one_liners.next_page()
printer.print_page(python_one_liners)
# ... Page Content 1 ...
```

*Listing 4-16: Adhering to the single responsibility principle*

The code in Listing 4-16 accomplishes the same task, but it satisfies the single responsibility principle. You create both a Book ❶ and a Printer ❸ class. The Book class represents book metadata and the current page number ❷, while the Printer class is responsible for printing the book to the device. You pass the book for which you want to print the current page into the method Printer.print_page() ❹. This way, data modeling (*what is the data?*) and data presentation (*how is the data presented to the user?*) are decoupled, and the code becomes easier to maintain. For example, if you wanted to change the book data model by adding a new attribute publishing_year, you'd do it in the class Book. And if you wanted to reflect this change in the data presentation by providing readers this information as well, you'd do so in the class Printer.

### Principle 11: Test

Test-driven development is an integral part of modern software development. No matter how skilled you are, you will make mistakes in your code. In order to catch them, you'll need to run periodic tests or build test-driven code in the first place. Every great software company employs multiple levels of testing before it ships the final product to the public, since it's far better to discover errors internally than to learn about them from unhappy users.

While there are no limitations to what types of tests you can perform to improve your software applications, these are the most common types:

**Unit tests**   With unit tests, you write a separate application to check the correct input/output relationship for different inputs of each function in the application. The unit tests are usually applied at regular intervals—for example, each time a new software version is released. This reduces the likelihood that a software change will cause previously stable features to suddenly fail.

**User acceptance tests**   These allow people in your target market to use your application in a controlled environment while you observe their behavior. You then ask them how they liked the application and how to improve it. These tests are usually deployed in the final phase of project development after extensive testing within the organization.

**Smoke tests**   Smoke tests are rough tests designed to try to fail the application under development before the teams building the software give the application to the testing team. In other words, smoke tests are often deployed by the application-building team for quality assurance before handing the code to the testing teams. When the app passes the smoke test, it's ready for the next round of testing.

**Performance tests**   Performance tests aim to show whether the application meets or even exceeds its users' performance requirements rather than testing the actual functionality. For instance, before Netflix releases a new feature, it must test its website for page-loading time. If the new feature slows down the frontend too much, Netflix doesn't release it, proactively avoiding a negative user experience.

**Scalability tests**   If your application becomes successful, you may have to handle 1,000 requests per minute instead of the original 2 requests. A scalability test will show whether your application is scalable enough to handle that. Note that a performant application isn't necessarily scalable and vice versa. For instance, a speed boat is very performant but doesn't scale to thousands of people at a time!

Testing and refactoring will often reduce complexity and the number of errors in your code. However, be careful not to over-engineer (see Principle 14)—you need to test scenarios that can occur only in the real world. For example, testing whether the Netflix application can handle 100 billion streaming devices is unnecessary considering there are only 7 billion potential viewers on the planet.

## Principle 12: Small Is Beautiful

*Small code* is code that requires only a relatively small number of lines to accomplish a single specified task. Here's an example of a small code function that reads an integer value from a user and ensures the input is indeed an integer:

```
def read_int(query):
    print(query)
    print('Please type an integer next:')
    try:
        x = int(input())
    except:
        print('Try again - type an integer!')
        return read_int(query)
    return x

print(read_int('Your age?'))
```

The code runs until the user types in an integer. Here's an example run:

```
Your age?
Please type an integer next:
hello
Try again - type an integer!
Your age?
Please type an integer next:
twenty
Try again - type an integer!
Your age?
Please type an integer next:
20
20
```

By separating the logic of reading an integer value from a user, you can reuse the same function multiple times. But, more importantly, you've broken up the code into smaller units of functionality that are relatively easy to read and understand.

Instead, many beginner coders (or lazy intermediate coders) write large, monolithic code functions, or so-called *God objects*, that do everything in a centralized manner. These monolithic code blocks are a nightmare to maintain. For one thing, it's easier for humans to understand one small code function at a time than to try to integrate a specific feature into a 10,000-line code block. You can potentially make far more mistakes in a large code block than in a few small functions and code blocks that you can then integrate with your existing codebase.

At the beginning of this chapter, Figure 4-1 showed that writing code becomes more time-consuming with each additional line, though writing clean code is much faster in the long run than writing dirty code. Figure 4-2 compares the time it takes to work with small code blocks versus monolithic code blocks. For large code blocks, the time it takes to add each additional line will increase superlinearly. If you stack multiple small code functions on top of each other, however, the time spent per additional line increases quasi-linearly. To best achieve this effect, you'll need to be sure each code function is more or less independent of other code functions. You'll learn more about this idea in the next principle, the Law of Demeter.

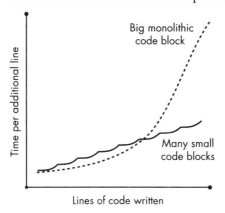

Figure 4-2: With the Big Monolithic Code Block, time increases exponentially. With the Many Small Code Blocks, time increases quasi-linearly.

## Principle 13: The Law of Demeter

Dependencies are everywhere. When you import a library in your code, your code depends partially on the library's functionality, but it will also have interdependencies within itself. In object-oriented programming, one function may depend on another function, one object on another object, and one class definition on another class definition.

To write clean code, minimize the interdependency of your code elements by following the *Law of Demeter*, which was proposed in the late 1980s by Ian Holland, a software developer working on a software project named after Demeter, the Greek goddess of agriculture, growth, and fertility. The project group promoted the idea of "growing software" as opposed to simply building it. However, what became known as the Law of Demeter has little to do with these arguably more metaphysic ideas—it's a practical approach of writing loosely coupled code in object-oriented programming. Here's a concise quote explaining the Law of Demeter from the project group's website, *http://ccs.neu.edu/home/lieber/what-is-demeter.html*:

> An important concept of Demeter is to split software into at least two parts: The first part defines the objects. The second part defines the operations. The goal of Demeter is to maintain a loose coupling between the objects and the operations, so that one can make modifications to either without serious impact on the other. This cuts down significantly on maintenance time.

In other words, you should minimize the dependencies of your code objects. By reducing dependencies between code objects, you reduce the complexity of your code and, in turn, improve maintainability. One specific implication is that every object should call only its own methods or methods from adjacent objects rather than call methods of objects it obtains from calling a method of an adjacent object. For the sake of explanation, let's define two objects A and B as *friends* if A calls a method provided by B. Simple. But what if B's method returns a reference to object C? Now, object A may perform something like this: B.method_of_B().method_of_C(). This is called *chaining* of method calls—in our metaphor, you talk to a friend of your friend. The Law of Demeter says to *talk only to your immediate friends*, so it discourages this type of method chaining. This may sound confusing at first, so let's dive into the practical example shown in Figure 4-3.

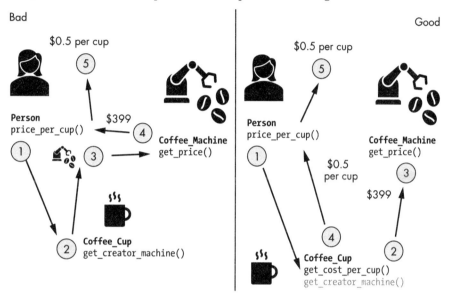

Figure 4-3: Law of Demeter: talking only to your friends to minimize dependencies

Figure 4-3 shows two object-oriented code projects that calculate the price per cup of coffee for a given person. One of the implementations violates the Law of Demeter, and the other one adheres to it. Let's start with the negative example first in which you use method chaining in the Person class to talk to a stranger ❶ (see Listing 4-17).

```
# VIOLATE LAW OF DEMETER (BAD)

class Person:
    def __init__(self, coffee_cup):
        self.coffee_cup = coffee_cup

    def price_per_cup(self):
        cups = 798
    ❶ machine_price = self.coffee_cup.get_creator_machine().get_price()
        return machine_price / cups


class Coffee_Machine:
    def __init__(self, price):
```

```
            self.price = price

        def get_price(self):
            return self.price


class Coffee_Cup:
    def __init__(self, machine):
        self.machine = machine

    def get_creator_machine(self):
        return self.machine


m = Coffee_Machine(399)
c = Coffee_Cup(m)
p = Person(c)

print('Price per cup:', p.price_per_cup())
# 0.5
```

*Listing 4-17: Code that violates the Law of Demeter*

You create the method price_per_cup() that calculates the cost per cup of coffee based on the price of the coffee machine and the number of cups produced by this machine. The Coffee_Cup object collects information about the price of the coffee machine, which influences the price per cup, and passes it to the caller of the method price_per_cup() on the Person object.

The diagram on the left of Figure 4-3 shows a bad strategy for doing so. Let's look at the step-by-step explanation of the corresponding code from Listing 4-17.

1.  The method price_per_cup() calls the method Coffee_Cup.get_creator _machine() to get a reference to the Coffee_Machine object that created the coffee.

2.  The method get_creator_machine() returns an object reference to the Coffee_Machine object that has produced the cup's contents.

3.  The method price_per_cup() calls the method Coffee_Machine.get_price() on the Coffee_Machine object it just obtained from the previous Coffee_Cup method call.

4.  The method get_price() returns the price of the machine.

5.  The method price_per_cup() calculates the depreciation per cup and uses this to estimate the price of a single cup. This is returned to the caller of the method.

This is a bad strategy because the class Person depends on two objects: Coffee_Cup and Coffee_Machine ❶. A programmer responsible for maintaining this class must know about both parent class definitions—any change in either of those may impact the Person class as well.

The Law of Demeter minimizes such dependencies. You can see a better way to model the same problem on the right in Figure 4-3 and in

Listing 4-18. In this code snippet, the `Person` class doesn't talk to the `Machine` class directly—it doesn't even need to be aware of its existence!

```
# ADHERE TO LAW OF DEMETER (GOOD)

class Person:
    def __init__(self, coffee_cup):
        self.coffee_cup = coffee_cup

    def price_per_cup(self):
        cups = 798
    ❶ return self.coffee_cup.get_cost_per_cup(cups)


class Coffee_Machine:
    def __init__(self, price):
        self.price = price

    def get_price(self):
        return self.price


class Coffee_Cup:
    def __init__(self, machine):
        self.machine = machine

    def get_creator_machine(self):
        return self.machine

    def get_cost_per_cup(self, cups):
        return self.machine.get_price() / cups


m = Coffee_Machine(399)
c = Coffee_Cup(m)
p = Person(c)

print('Price per cup:', p.price_per_cup())
# 0.5
```

*Listing 4-18: Code that adheres to the Law of Demeter by not talking to strangers*

Let's examine this code in a step-by-step manner:

1. The method `price_per_cup()` calls the method `Coffee_Cup.get_cost_per_cup()` to get the estimated price per cup.

2. The method `get_cost_per_cup()`—before replying to the calling method— calls the method `Coffee_Machine.get_price()` to access the price of the machine.

3. The method `get_price()` returns the price information.

4. The method `get_cost_per_cup()` calculates the price per cup and returns it to the calling method `price_per_cup()`.

5. The method `price_per_cup()` simply forwards this calculated value to its caller ❶.

This is a better approach, because the class `Person` is now independent of the class `Coffee_Machine`. The total number of dependencies is reduced. For a project with hundreds of classes, reducing dependencies dramatically reduces the overall complexity of your application. Here's the danger in terms of growing complexity for large applications: the number of potential dependencies grows superlinearly with the number of objects. Roughly speaking, a superlinear curve grows faster than a straight line. For example, doubling the number of objects can easily quadruple the number of dependencies (which equates to complexity). However, following the Law of Demeter can offset this trend by significantly reducing the number of dependencies. If every object talks to only $k$ other objects and you have $n$ objects, the total number of dependencies is bounded by $k*n$, which is a linear relationship if $k$ is a constant. Thus, the Law of Demeter can mathematically help you gracefully scale your applications!

## Principle 14: You Ain't Gonna Need It

This principle suggests that you should never implement code if you only *suspect* that you'll need to use it someday in the future—because you ain't gonna need it! Write code only if you're 100 percent sure it's necessary. Code for today's needs and not tomorrow's. If in the future you actually need the code you previously only suspected you needed, you can still implement the feature then. But in the meantime, you've saved many unnecessary lines of code.

It helps to think from first principles: the simplest and cleanest code is the empty file. Now, go from there—what do you *need* to add to that? In Chapter 3, you learned about the MVP: code that is stripped of features to focus on the core functionality. If you minimize the number of features you pursue, you'll obtain cleaner and simpler code than you could ever attain through refactoring methods or all other principles combined. Consider leaving out features that provide relatively little value compared to others. Opportunity costs are seldom measured but are often significant. You should really *need* a feature before you even consider implementing it.

An implication of this is to avoid *overengineering*: creating a product that is more performant and robust or contains more features than needed. It adds unnecessary complexity, which should immediately ring your alarm bells.

For example, I've often encountered problems that could be solved within a few minutes using a naive algorithmic approach but, like many programmers, I refused to accept the minor limitations of these algorithms. Instead, I studied state-of-the-art clustering algorithms to eke out a few percentage points of clustering performance compared to the simple KMeans algorithm. These long-tail optimizations were incredibly costly—I had to spend 80 percent of the time to obtain 20 percent of the improvement. This would have been unavoidable if I'd *needed* that 20 percent and had no other way to get it, but in reality, I didn't need to implement fancy clustering algorithms. A typical case of overengineering!

Always go for the low-hanging fruit first. Use naive algorithms and straightforward methods to establish a benchmark, then analyze which new feature or performance optimization would yield superior results for the overall application. Think global, not local: focus on the big picture (as per Principle 1) rather than on small, time-consuming fixes.

## Principle 15: Don't Use Too Many Levels of Indentation

Most programming languages use text indentation to visualize the hierarchical structure of potentially nested conditional blocks, function definitions, or code loops. Overusing indentation, however, can decrease the readability of your code. Listing 4-19 shows an example of a code snippet with too many levels of indentation, which makes it hard to quickly understand.

```
def if_confusion(x, y):
    if x>y:
        if x-5>0:
            x = y
            if y==y+y:
                return "A"
            else:
                return "B"
        elif x+y>0:
            while x>y:
                x = x-1
            while y>x:
                y = y-1
            if x==y:
                return "E"
        else:
            x = 2 * x
            if x==y:
                return "F"
            else:
                return "G"
    else:
        if x-2>y-4:
            x_old = x
            x = y * y
            y = 2 * x_old
            if (x-4)**2>(y-7)**2:
                return "C"
            else:
                return "D"
        else:
            return "H"

print(if_confusion(2, 8))
```

Listing 4-19: Too many levels of nested code blocks

If you now try to guess the output of this code snippet, you'll find it's actually difficult to trace. The code function if_confusion(x, y) performs relatively simple checks on variables x and y. However, it's easy to get lost in the different levels of indentation. The code is not clean at all.

Listing 4-20 shows how to write the same code more cleanly and simply.

```
def if_confusion(x,y):
    if x>y and x>5 and y==0:
        return "A"
    if x>y and x>5:
        return "B"
    if x>y and x+y>0:
        return "E"
    if x>y and 2*x==y:
        return "F"
    if x>y:
        return "G"
    if x>y-2 and (y*y-4)**2>(2*x-7)**2:
        return "C"
    if x>y-2:
        return "D"
    return "H"
```

*Listing 4-20: Fewer levels of nested code blocks*

In Listing 4-20, we reduced indentation and nesting. You can now go over all checks and see what applies first to your two arguments x and y. Most coders will enjoy reading flat code much more than reading highly nested code—even if it comes at the expense of redundant checks; here, for example, x>y is checked multiple times.

## Principle 16: Use Metrics

Use code quality metrics to track the complexity of your code over time. The ultimate, if informal, metric is known as the number of WTFs per minute, intended to measure your code readers' frustration. The results will be low for clean and simple code and high for dirty, confusing code.

As a proxy for this hard-to-quantify standard, you can use established metrics such as the NPath complexity or cyclomatic complexity discussed in Chapter 1. For most IDEs, many online tools and plug-ins will automatically calculate the complexity as you write your source code. These include CyclomaticComplexity, which you can find by searching in the plug-ins section of JetBrains at *https://plugins.jetbrains.com/*. In my experience, the actual measure of complexity used is less important than being aware of the fact that you need to weed out complexity wherever you can. I highly recommend using these tools to help you write cleaner and simpler code. The return on your invested time will be phenomenal.

## Principle 17: Boy Scout Rule and Refactoring

The boy scout rule is simple: *leave the campground cleaner than you found it.* It's a great rule to live and code by. Get into the habit of cleaning up every piece of code you encounter. This will not only improve the codebases you're involved in and make your own life easier but also help you develop the sharp eye of a master coder who can evaluate source code quickly. As a bonus, it'll help your team be more productive, and your colleagues will be grateful for your value-oriented attitude. Note that this shouldn't violate the rule we stated earlier about avoiding premature optimization (overengineering). Spending time to clean up your code to reduce complexity is almost always efficient. Doing so will yield big dividends in reduced maintenance overhead, bugs, and cognitive demands. Put succinctly, overengineering is likely to *increase* complexity whereas cleaning up the code will *reduce* complexity.

The process of improving your code is called *refactoring*. You could argue that refactoring is the overall method comprising every principle we've discussed here. As a great coder, you'll incorporate many of the clean code principles from the beginning. Even then, however, you'll still need to occasionally refactor your code to clean up any messes you've made. In particular, you should refactor your code before releasing any new features to keep the code clean.

There are many techniques for refactoring code. One is to explain your code to a colleague or have them look it over in order to discover any poor decisions you've made and had not noticed on your own. For example, you may have created two classes, Cars and Trucks, because you expected your application would need to model both. As you explain your code to your teammate, you realize that you don't use the class Trucks very often—and when you do, you use methods that already exist in the Car class. Your colleague suggests creating a Vehicle class that handles all cars and trucks. This allows you to get rid of many lines of code immediately. This type of thinking can result in enormous improvements, since it will force you to account for your decisions and explain your project from a bird's-eye view.

If you're an introverted coder, you can explain your code to a rubber duck instead—a technique known as *rubber duck debugging*.

Beyond speaking to your colleagues (or your rubber duck), you can use the other clean code principles listed here to quickly evaluate your code from time to time. When you do, you'll likely discover some tweaks you can apply quickly to greatly reduce complexity by cleaning up your codebase. This integral part of your software development process will improve your results significantly.

## Conclusion

In this chapter, you've learned 17 principles for how to write clean and simple code. You've learned that clean code reduces complexity and increases your productivity as well as the scalability and maintainability of your project. You've learned that you should use libraries wherever possible to reduce clutter and increase your code quality. You've learned that choosing meaningful names of variables and functions while adhering to standards is important to reduce friction for future readers of your code. You've learned to design functions to do one thing only. Reducing complexity and increasing scalability by minimizing dependencies (according to the Law of Demeter) can be done by avoiding direct and indirect method chaining. You've learned to comment code in a way that provides a valuable glimpse into your mind, but you've also learned to avoid unnecessary or trivial comments. And, most importantly, you've learned that the key to unlocking your clean code superpower is to code for humans, not machines.

You can gradually improve your clean code–writing skills by collaborating with great coders, reading their code on GitHub, and studying the best practices in your programming language. Integrate a linter that dynamically checks your code against those best practices into your programming environment. From time to time, revisit these clean code principles and check your current project against them.

In the next chapter, you'll learn another principle of effective coding that goes beyond just writing clean code: premature optimization. You'll be surprised by how much time and effort is wasted by programmers who haven't yet figured out that *premature optimization is the root of all evil*!

# 5

## PREMATURE OPTIMIZATION IS THE ROOT OF ALL EVIL

In this chapter, you'll learn how premature optimization can hinder your productivity. *Premature optimization* is the act of spending valuable resources—time, effort, lines of code—on unnecessary code optimizations, especially before you have all the relevant information. It is one of the main problems with poorly written code. Premature optimization comes in many flavors; this chapter will introduce some of the most relevant ones. We'll study practical examples showing where premature optimization occurs that will be relevant for your own code projects. We'll close the chapter with actionable tips on performance tuning, ensuring that it is *not* premature.

### Six Types of Premature Optimization

There's nothing wrong with optimized code per se, but it always comes with a cost, whether that's additional programming time or extra lines of code. When you optimize code snippets, you're generally trading complexity for performance. Sometimes you can obtain both low complexity and high performance, for example, by writing clean code, but you must spend programming time to accomplish this! If you do this too early in the process, you'll often spend time optimizing code that may never be used in practice or that has little impact on the overall runtime of the program. You'll also optimize without having enough information about when the code is called and possible input values. Wasting precious resources like programming time and code lines can reduce your productivity by orders of magnitude, so it's important to know how to invest in them wisely.

But don't take my word for it. Here's what one of the most influential computer scientists of all time, Donald Knuth, says about premature optimization:

> Programmers waste enormous amounts of time thinking about, or worrying about, the speed of noncritical parts of their programs, and these attempts at efficiency actually have a strong negative impact when debugging and maintenance are considered. We should forget about small efficiencies, say about 97% of the time: premature optimization is the root of all evil.[1]

Premature optimization can take many forms, so to explore the issue, we'll look at six common cases I've encountered in which you too might be tempted to prematurely focus on small efficiencies, slowing your progress.

## Optimizing Code Functions

Be wary of spending time optimizing functions before you know how much those functions will be used. Say you encounter a function you just cannot stand to leave unoptimized. You reason to yourself that it's bad programming style to use naive methods and that you should use more efficient data structures or algorithms to tackle the problem. You dive into research mode and spend hours researching and fine-tuning algorithms. But as it turns out, this function is executed only a few times in the final project: the optimization doesn't result in meaningful performance improvements.

## Optimizing Features

Avoid adding features that aren't strictly necessary and wasting time optimizing those features. Suppose you develop a smartphone app that translates text into Morse code, expressed by blinking lights. You've learned in Chapter 3 that implementing an MVP first, rather than creating a polished end product with many, possibly unnecessary, features, is the best way to go. In this case, the MVP would be a simple app with one function: translate text into Morse code by providing a text via a simple input form and hitting a button on which the app then translates this text to Morse code. However, you think the MVP rule doesn't apply to your

---

1. "Structured Programming with *go to* Statements," *ACM Computing Surveys* 6, no. 1 (1974).

project and decide to add a few extra features: a text-to-audio converter and a receiver that translates light signals to text. After shipping your app, you learn that your users never use these features. Premature optimization has significantly slowed down your product development cycle and delayed your ability to incorporate user feedback.

## Optimizing Planning

If you prematurely optimize the planning phase, trying to find solutions to problems that haven't yet occurred, you risk delaying your ability to receive valuable feedback. While you certainly shouldn't avoid planning entirely, getting stuck in the planning phase can be just as costly. To ship something of value to the real world, you must accept imperfection. You need user feedback and sanity checks from testers to figure out where to focus. Planning can help you avoid certain pitfalls, but if you're not taking action, you'll never finish your project and will remain stuck in the ivory tower of theory.

## Optimizing Scalability

Prematurely optimizing the scalability of your application before you have a realistic idea of the audience can be a major distractor and can easily cost you tens of thousands of dollars' worth of developer and server time. Expecting millions of users, you design a distributed architecture that dynamically adds virtual machines to handle peak load if necessary. However, creating distributed systems is a complex and error-prone task that may easily take you months to implement. Many projects fail anyway; if you do become as successful as your wildest dreams suggest, you'll have plenty of opportunity to scale your system with the increase of demand. Worse, the distribution may *reduce* an application's scalability, due to an increased communication and data consistency overhead. Scalable distributed systems come at a price—are you sure you need to pay it? Don't try to scale to millions of users before you've served your first one.

## Optimizing Test Design

Optimizing for tests too soon is also a major driver of wasted developer time. Test-driven development has many zealous followers who misinterpret the idea of *implementing tests before functionality* to always write tests first—even if the purpose of a code function is pure experimentation or the code function doesn't lend itself well to testing in the first place. To write experimental code is to test concepts and ideas, and adding another layer of tests to experimental code can harm progress and does not adhere to the philosophy of rapid prototyping. In addition, suppose you believe in rigorous test-driven development and insist on 100 percent test coverage. Some functions—for instance, those that process free text from users—don't work very well with unit tests because of their unpredictable human-based input. For those functions, only real human beings can test them in a meaningful way—in these cases, real-world users *are* the only test that matters. Nevertheless, you prematurely optimize for a perfect coverage of unit tests. This approach has little value: it slows down the software development cycle while introducing unnecessary complexity.

### Optimizing Object-Oriented World Building

Object-oriented approaches can often introduce major unnecessary complexity and premature "conceptual" optimization. Suppose you want to model your application's world using a complex hierarchy of classes. You write a small game about car racing. You create a class hierarchy where the Porsche class inherits from the Car class, which inherits from the Vehicle class. After all, every Porsche is a car, and every car is a vehicle. However, the multi-level class hierarchy leads to complexity in your codebase, and future programmers have trouble figuring out what your code does. In many cases, these types of stacked inheritance structures add unnecessary complexity. Avoid them by using the ideas of MVPs: start with the simplest model and extend it only if needed. Don't optimize your code to model a world with more details than the application actually needs.

## Premature Optimization: A Story

Now that you have a general sense of the problems premature optimization can cause, let's write a small Python application and see in real time how premature optimization adds unnecessary complexity to the code of a small transaction-tracking application that doesn't need to scale gracefully to thousands of users.

Alice, Bob, and Carl play poker each Friday night. After a few rounds, they decide that they need to develop a system to keep track of the money each player owes after a given game night. Alice is a passionate programmer and creates a small application that tracks the players' balances, shown in Listing 5-1.

```
transactions = []
balances = {}


❶ def transfer(sender, receiver, amount):
      transactions.append((sender, receiver, amount))
      if not sender in balances:
          balances[sender] = 0
      if not receiver in balances:
          balances[receiver] = 0
    ❷ balances[sender] -= amount
      balances[receiver] += amount

def get_balance(user):
    return balances[user]
```

```
def max_transaction():
    return max(transactions, key=lambda x:x[2])


❸ transfer('Alice', 'Bob', 2000)
❹ transfer('Bob', 'Carl', 4000)
❺ transfer('Alice', 'Carl', 2000)

  print('Balance Alice: ' + str(get_balance('Alice')))
  print('Balance Bob: ' + str(get_balance('Bob')))
  print('Balance Carl: ' + str(get_balance('Carl')))

  print('Max Transaction: ' + str(max_transaction()))

❻ transfer('Alice', 'Bob', 1000)
❼ transfer('Carl', 'Alice', 8000)

  print('Balance Alice: ' + str(get_balance('Alice')))
  print('Balance Bob: ' + str(get_balance('Bob')))
  print('Balance Carl: ' + str(get_balance('Carl')))

  print('Max Transaction: ' + str(max_transaction()))
```

*Listing 5-1: A simple script to track transactions and balances*

The script has two global variables, transactions and balances. The list transactions tracks the transactions between players as they occur during a game night. Each transaction is a tuple of the sender identifier, the receiver identifier, and the amount to be transferred from sender to receiver ❶. The dictionary balances tracks a player's current balance: a dictionary that maps a user identifier to the number of credits of that user based on the transactions so far ❷.

The function transfer(sender, receiver, amount) creates and stores a new transaction in the global list, creates new balances for the sender and receiver if they don't already exist, and updates the balances according to the given amount. The function get_balance(user) returns the balance of the user given as an argument, and max_transaction() goes over all transactions and returns the one that has the maximum value in the third tuple element, the transaction amount.

Initially all balances are zero. The application transfers 2,000 units from Alice to Bob ❸, 4,000 units from Bob to Carl ❹, and 2,000 units from Alice to Carl ❺. At this point, Alice owes 4,000 (with a negative balance of –4,000), Bob owes 2,000, and Carl has 6,000 units. After printing the maximum transaction, Alice transfers 1,000 units to Bob ❻, and Carl transfers 8,000 units to Alice ❼. Now, the accounts have changed: Alice has 3,000, Bob –1,000, and Carl –2,000 units. In particular, the application returns the following output:

```
Balance Alice: -4000
Balance Bob: -2000
Balance Carl: 6000
Max Transaction: ('Bob', 'Carl', 4000)
```

```
Balance Alice: 3000
Balance Bob: -1000
Balance Carl: -2000
Max Transaction: ('Carl', 'Alice', 8000)
```

But Alice isn't happy with the application. She realizes that calling max_transaction() results in redundant calculations—because the function is called twice, the script goes over the list transactions twice to find the transaction with the maximum amount. But when calculating max_transaction() the second time, it partially performs the same calculations again by going through all the transactions to find the maximum—including those for which it already knows the maximum, that is, the first three transactions ❸–❺. Alice correctly sees some *optimization potential* by introducing a new variable, max_transaction, that keeps track of the maximum transaction seen so far whenever a new transaction is created.

Listing 5-2 shows the three lines of code Alice added to implement this change.

```
transactions = []
balances = {}
max_transaction = ('X', 'Y', float('-Inf'))


def transfer(sender, receiver, amount):
...
    if amount > max_transaction[2]:
        max_transaction = (sender, receiver, amount)
```

*Listing 5-2: Applied optimization to reduce redundant computations*

The variable max_transaction maintains the maximum transaction amount among all transactions seen so far. Thus, there's no need for the maximum to be recomputed after every game night. Initially, you set the maximum transaction value to negative infinity so that the first real transaction will definitely be larger. Each time a new transaction is added, the program compares that new transaction to the current maximum, and if it is larger, the current transaction becomes the current maximum. Without the optimization, if you called the function max_transaction() 1,000 times on a list of 1,000 transactions, you'd have to perform 1,000,000 comparisons to find 1,000 maxima because you traversed the list of 1,000 elements 1,000 times (1,000 * 1,000 = 1,000,000). With the optimization, you'd need to retrieve the currently stored value in max_transaction only once for each function call. As the list has 1,000 elements, you need at most 1,000 operations to maintain the current maximum. This leads to a reduction of three orders of magnitude in the number of operations needed.

Many coders cannot resist implementing such optimizations, but their complexity adds up. In Alice's case, she'll soon have to keep track of a handful of additional variables to track additional statistics her friends might be interested in: min_transaction, avg_transaction, median_transaction, and alice_max_transaction (to track her own maximum transaction value). Each injects a few more lines of code into the project, increasing the likelihood a bug will appear. If Alice forgets to update a variable at the proper location, for instance, she'll have to spend precious time fixing it. Even worse, she may miss the bug entirely, resulting in a corrupted balance of Alice's account and a few hundreds of dollars of damage. Her friends might even suspect that Alice wrote the code in her favor! This final point may sound a little tongue-in-cheek, but in real-world cases, the stakes are higher. Second-order consequences can be even more severe than the more predictable first-order consequences of complexity.

All these potential problems could have been averted had Alice refrained from applying a *potential optimization* without fully thinking through whether this optimization was premature. The goal of the app is to broker one evening's transaction between three friends. Realistically, there will be at most a few hundred transactions and a dozen calls to `max_transaction` rather than the thousands for which the optimized code is designed. Alice's computer could've executed the unoptimized code within a split second, and neither Bob nor Carl would even have realized that the code was unoptimized. Plus, the unoptimized code is simpler and easier to maintain.

However, suppose word gets around and a casino—which relies on high performance, scalability, and long-term transaction histories—contacts Alice to implement the same system. In that case, she can still fix the bottleneck of recomputing the maximum instead of tracking it quickly. But now she'd be certain that the additional code complexity was indeed a good investment. By avoiding optimization until the application requires it, she'd have saved herself dozens of those unnecessary premature optimizations.

## Six Tips for Performance Tuning

Alice's story not only gave us a detailed picture of premature optimization in practice but also hinted at the proper way to successfully optimize. It's important to remember that Donald Knuth did not argue that optimization *itself* is the root of all evil. Instead, the real problem is *premature* optimization. Now that Knuth's quote has become quite popular, many mistakenly take it to be an argument against all optimization. When it comes at the right time, however, optimization can be critical.

The rapid technological improvements in recent decades are largely due to optimizations: circuit placement on chips, algorithms, and software usability have been optimized continuously over time. Moore's law states that the improvements in computer chip technology that make computing incredibly cheap and efficient will continue exponentially for a long time yet. Improvements in chip technology have significant potential, and they cannot be considered premature. If they create value for many, optimizations are at the heart of progress.

As a rule of thumb, you should optimize only if you have clear evidence—such as measurements from performance optimization tools—that the code part or function to be optimized is indeed one of the bottlenecks and that users of the application will appreciate or even demand a better performance. Optimizing the speed of starting the Windows operating system is not premature because it'll directly benefit millions of users, whereas optimizing the scalability of your web application with an upper limit of 1,000 users per month, who are only requesting a static website, is premature. The costs of *developing* an application are not as high as the costs of thousands of users *using* it. If you can spend one hour of your time to save the users a few seconds, it's usually a win! Your users' time is more valuable than your own. This is why we use computers in the first place—to invest a few resources upfront and gain many more resources afterward. Optimization is not always premature. Sometimes, you must optimize in order to create a valuable product in the first place—why bother shipping an unoptimized product that doesn't generate any value? Having seen several reasons to avoid premature optimization, we will now look at six performance tips to help you choose how and when to optimize your code.

## Measure First, Improve Second

Measure your software's performance so you know where it can and should be improved. What you don't measure can't be improved, since you have no way to track your progress.

Premature optimization is often an optimization applied before you've even measured, which is the direct basis of the idea that premature optimization is the root of all evil. You should always optimize only after you have begun to measure the performance of your non-optimized code, like memory footprint or speed. This is your benchmark. There's no point in trying to improve runtime, for example, if you don't know what your original runtime is. There's no way to tell if your "optimization" actually increases total runtime or results in no measurable effect unless you begin with a clear benchmark.

As a general strategy for measuring performance, start with writing the most straightforward, naive code possible that's also easy to read. You may call this your *prototype*, the *naive approach*, or the *MVP*. Document your measurements in a spreadsheet. This is your first benchmark. Create an alternative code solution and measure its performance against the benchmark. Once you've rigorously proven that your optimization improves your code performance, the new optimized code becomes your new benchmark, which all subsequent improvements should be able to beat. If an optimization doesn't measurably improve your code, throw it away.

This way, you can track your code's improvement over time. You can also document, prove, and defend an optimization to your boss, your peer group, or even the scientific community.

## Pareto Is King

The 80/20 principle, or *Pareto principle*, discussed in Chapter 2, also applies to performance optimization. Some features will take up considerably more resources, such as time and memory footprint, than others, so focusing on improving bottlenecks like these will help you effectively optimize your code.

To exemplify the high degree of imbalance of different processes running in parallel on my operating system, take a look at my current central processing unit (CPU) usage in Figure 5-1.

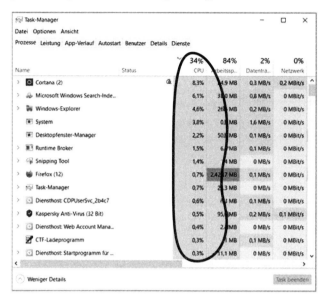

Figure 5-1: Unequal distribution of the CPU demand of different applications running on a Windows PC

If you plot this in Python, you see a Pareto-like distribution, as shown in Figure 5-2.

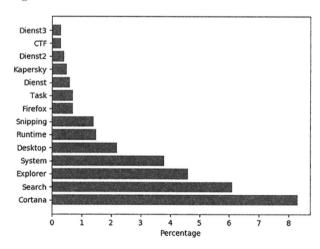

Figure 5-2: CPU usage of different applications on a Windows PC

A small percentage of application code requires a significant percentage of CPU usage. If I want to reduce the CPU usage on my computer, I just need to close Cortana and Search and—voilà—a significant portion of the CPU load disappears, shown in Figure 5-3.

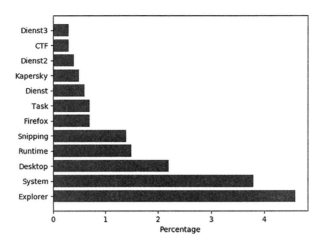

Figure 5-3: The results after "optimizing" a Windows system by closing not-needed applications

Removing the two most expensive tasks reduces the CPU load considerably, but notice that the new plot looks similar to the first at a glance: two tasks, this time Explorer and System, are still much more expensive than the rest. This demonstrates an important rule of performance tuning: performance optimization is fractal. As soon as you've removed one bottleneck, you'll find another bottleneck lurking around. Bottlenecks will always be in any system, but if you repeatedly remove them as they appear, you'll get maximal "bang for your buck." In a practical code project, you'll see the same distribution of a relatively small number of functions taking the majority of the resources (for example, CPU cycles). Often you can focus your optimization effort on the bottleneck function that takes the most resources, such as by rewriting it with more sophisticated algorithms or thinking about ways to avoid the computation (for example, caching of intermediate results). Of course, the next bottleneck will appear right after you've resolved the current one; that's why you need to measure your code and decide when it's time to stop optimizing. For example, it doesn't make a lot of sense to improve the response time of a web application from 2 ms to 1 ms when the user wouldn't perceive the difference anyway. Due to the fractal nature of optimizations and the Pareto principle (see Chapter 2), obtaining these small gains often requires a lot of effort and developer time and may yield little gain in terms of usability or application utility.

## Algorithmic Optimization Wins

Say you've decided your code needs a particular optimization because user feedback and statistics indicate that your application is too slow. You've measured your current speed in seconds or bytes and know the target speed you're aiming for, and you've found your bottleneck. Your next step is to figure out how to overcome that bottleneck.

Many bottlenecks can be resolved by tuning your *algorithms and data structures*. For example, imagine you're developing a financial application. You know your bottleneck is the function `calculate_ROI()`, which goes over all combinations of potential buying and selling points to calculate the maximum profit. As this function is the bottleneck of the entire application, you want to find a better algorithm for it. After a bit of research, you find out about the *maximum profit algorithm*, a simple, powerful replacement that will speed up your computation significantly. The same research can be done on data structures causing bottlenecks.

To reduce bottlenecks and optimize performance, ask yourself:

- Can you find better algorithms that are already proven—for example, in books, research papers, or even Wikipedia?

- Can you tweak existing algorithms for your specific problem?

- Can you improve the data structures? Some common easy solutions include using sets instead of lists (checking membership, for example, is much faster for sets than lists) or dictionaries instead of collections of tuples.

Spending time researching these questions pays off both for your application and for you. You'll become a better computer scientist in the process.

## All Hail the Cache

Once you've made any necessary changes based on the previous tips, you can move on to this quick and dirty trick for removing unnecessary computations: store the result of a subset of computations you have already performed in a cache. This trick works surprisingly well for a variety of applications. Before performing any new computation, you first check the cache to see if you've already done that computation. This is similar to how you approach simple calculations in your head—at a certain point, you don't *actually* calculate 6 * 5 in your head but simply rely on your memory to give you the result right away. Consequently, caching makes sense only if the same type of intermediate calculations appears multiple times throughout your application. Fortunately, this holds for most real-world applications—for example, thousands of users may watch the same YouTube video in a given day, so caching it close to the user (rather than thousands of miles away in a distant data center) saves scarce network bandwidth resources.

Let's explore a short code example where caching results in significant performance benefits: the Fibonacci algorithm.

```
def fib(n):
    if n < 2:
        return n
    fib_n = fib(n-1) + fib(n-2)
    return fib_n


print(fib(100))
```

This will output the result of repeatedly adding the last and second-last element of the series up to the 100th sequence element:

---

354224848179261915075

---

This algorithm is slow because the functions fib(n-1) and fib(n-2) calculate more or less the same things. For instance, both separately calculate the (n-3)th Fibonacci element instead of reusing each other's result for this computation. The redundancy adds up—even for this simple function call, the computation takes much too long.

One way to improve performance here is to create a cache. *Caching* allows you to store the results of previous computations, so in this case, fib2(n-3) is calculated only once, and when you need it again, you can instantly pull the result from the cache.

In Python, we can make a simple cache by creating a dictionary where you associate each function input (as an input string, for instance) with the function output. You can then ask the cache to give you the computations you've already performed.

Here's the caching variant of Python Fibonacci:

---

```
cache = dict()

def fib(n):
    if n in cache:
        return cache[n]
    if n < 2:
        return n
    fib_n = fib(n-1) + fib(n-2)
❶ cache[n] = fib_n
    return fib_n


print(fib(100))
# 354224848179261915075
```

---

You store the result of fib(n-1) + fib(n-2) in the cache ❶. If you already have the nth Fibonacci number result, you pull it from the cache rather than recalculating it again and again. On my machine, this increases the speed by almost 2,000 times when calculating the first 40 Fibonacci numbers!

There are two basic strategies for effective caching:

**Perform computations in advance ("offline") and store their results in the cache.**

This is a great strategy for web applications where you can fill up a large cache once, or once a day, and then serve the result of your pre-computations to the users. For them, your calculations seem blazingly fast. Mapping services heavily use this trick to speed up the shortest path computations.

**Perform computations as they appear ("online") and store their results in the cache.**

An example is an online Bitcoin address checker that sums all incoming transactions and deducts all outgoing transactions to compute the balance of a given Bitcoin address. Once done, it could cache the intermediate results for this address to avoid recomputing the same transactions once the same user checks again. This reactive form is the most basic form of caching, where you don't need to decide which computations to perform in advance.

In both cases, the more computations you store, the higher the likelihood of *cache hits* where the relevant computation can be returned immediately. However, as there's usually a memory limit on the number of cache entries you can save, you'll need a sensible *cache replacement policy*: as the cache has a limited size, it may fill up quickly. At that point, the cache can store a new value only by replacing an old value. A common replacement policy is *first in, first out (FIFO)*, which would replace the oldest cache entry with the new one. The best strategy depends on the concrete application, but FIFO is a good first bet.

## Less Is More

Is your problem too hard to be solved efficiently? Make it easier! It sounds obvious, but so many coders are perfectionists. They accept colossal complexity and computational overhead just to implement a small feature that may not even get recognized by users. Instead of optimizing, it's often much better to reduce complexity and get rid of unnecessary features and computations. Consider the problems faced by search engine developers, for example: "What is the perfect match for a given search query?" Finding the optimal solution for such a problem is extremely hard and involves searching billions of websites. However, search engines like Google don't solve the problem optimally; rather, they do the best they can in the time they have by using heuristics. Instead of checking billions of websites against a user search query, they focus on a couple of high-probability bets by using rough heuristics to estimate the quality of individual websites (such as the famous PageRank algorithm) and consult suboptimal websites if no other high-quality website answers the query. You too should use heuristics rather than optimal algorithms in most cases. Ask yourself the following questions: What is your current bottleneck calculating? Why does it exist? Is it worth the effort to solve the problem anyway? Can you remove the feature or offer a downsized version? If the feature is used by 1 percent of your users, but 100 percent perceive the increased latency, it may be time for some minimalism (removing the feature that is hardly used but provides a bad experience to those who use it).

To simplify your code, think about whether it makes sense to do one of the following:

- Remove your current bottleneck altogether by just skipping the feature.
- Simplify the problem by replacing it with a simpler version of the problem.
- Get rid of 1 expensive feature to add 10 cheap ones, in accordance with the 80/20 policy.
- Omit one important feature so that you can pursue an even more important one; think about opportunity costs.

### Know When to Stop

Performance optimization can be one of the most time-consuming aspects of coding. There's always room for improvement, but your effort needed to improve performance tends to increase once you have already exhausted the low-hanging fruit techniques. At some point, improving performance is just a waste of your time.

Ask yourself regularly: Is it worth the effort to keep optimizing? The answer can usually be found by studying the users of your application. What performance do they need? Do they even perceive the difference between the original and the optimized version of the application? Do some of them complain about bad performance? Answering these questions will give you a rough estimate of the maximum runtime of your application. Now, you can start optimizing bottlenecks until you reach this threshold. Then stop.

## Conclusion

In this chapter, you've learned why it's important to avoid premature optimization. An optimization is premature if it takes more value than it adds. Depending on the project, value can often be measured in terms of developer time, usability metrics, expected revenue of an app or feature, or its utility for a subgroup of users. For instance, if an optimization can save time or money for thousands of users, it is likely not premature, even if you must spend significant developer resources to optimize the codebase. However, if the optimization cannot lead to perceptible differences in the quality of the lives of the users or programmers, it most likely is premature. Yes, there are many more advanced models on the software-engineering process, but common sense and a general awareness of the dangers of premature optimization go a long way without you needing to study fancy books or research papers on software development models. For instance, a useful rule of thumb is to write readable and clean code to start with and not care too much about performance, then optimize the parts with a high expected value based on experience, hard facts from performance-tracking tools, and real-world results from user studies.

In the next chapter, you'll learn about the concept of flow—a programmer's best friend.

# 6

## FLOW

*Flow is the source code of ultimate human performance.*
—Steven Kotler

 In this chapter, you'll learn about the concept of flow and how you can use it to ramp up your programming productivity. Many programmers find themselves in office environments with constant interruptions, meetings, and other diversions that can make it nearly impossible to reach a pure state of productive programming. To gain more insight on what flow is and how to accomplish it in practice, we'll examine many examples throughout this chapter, but generally speaking, *flow* is a state of pure concentration and focus—what some people might call "being in the zone."

Flow is not a strictly programmatic concept but a state that can be applied to any task in any field. Here, we'll look at how you can go about attaining a state of flow and how it can be useful to you.

# What Is Flow?

The concept of flow was popularized by Mihaly Csikszentmihalyi (pronounced "chick-sent-me-high"), a distinguished professor of psychology and management at Claremont Graduate University and former head of the department of psychology at the University of Chicago. In 1990, Csikszentmihalyi published the groundbreaking book about his life's work titled, appropriately, *Flow*.

But what is flow? Let's start with the somewhat subjective definition of how it feels. Afterward, you'll learn a more tangible definition of flow based on what you can measure—as a coder, you'll like the second definition more!

Experiencing flow is being in a state of complete immersion in the task at hand: focused and concentrated. You forget about time; you're in the zone, hyper-aware. You might feel a sense of ecstasy, freed from all other burdens of everyday life. Your inner clarity increases, and it becomes evident to you what you need to be doing next—the activities flow naturally from one to another. Your confidence in your ability to complete the next activity is unshaken. Completing the activity is its own reward, and you enjoy every second. Both your performance and your results go through the roof.

According to psychological research led by Csikszentmihalyi, a state of flow has six components

**Attention**  You feel a deep sense of concentration and complete focus.

**Action**  You feel a bias toward action, and you move forward with your current task quickly and efficiently—your focused awareness helps drive the momentum. Every action feeds into the next action, creating a flow of successful actions.

**Self**  You become less aware of yourself, and you shut down your inner critics, doubts, and fears. You think less about yourself (*reflection*) and more about the task at hand (*action*). You lose yourself in the task at hand.

**Control**  Even as you're less self-aware, you enjoy an increased sense of control about the present situation, giving you calm confidence and allowing you to think outside the box and develop creative solutions.

**Time**  You lose the ability to experience time passing.

**Reward**  The labor of the activity is all you want to do; there may be no external reward, but being immersed in the activity is intrinsically rewarding in itself.

The terms *flow* and *attention* are closely related. In a 2013 dissertation on attention deficit hyperactivity disorder (ADHD), Rony Sklar points out that the term *attention deficit* wrongly implies that patients experiencing it cannot focus. Another term for flow is *hyperfocus*, and legions of psychology researchers (for example, Kaufmann et al. 2000) have proven that ADHD patients are quite capable of hyperfocus; they only struggle with sustaining attention for tasks that are not intrinsically rewarding. You don't need to get diagnosed with ADHD to know that it's hard to focus on things you don't enjoy doing.

But if you've ever completely lost yourself playing an exciting game, programming a fun application, or watching an interesting movie—you know how easy it is to reach flow if you like the activity. In a state of flow, your body releases five *feel-good* neurochemical pleasure drugs such as endorphins, dopamine, and serotonin. It's like experiencing the "benefits" of taking recreational drugs but without some of the negative consequences—even Csikszentmihalyi warned that flow can be addictive. Learning to enter a state of flow makes you smarter and more productive—if you manage to direct the flow activity into productive endeavors such as programming.

Now, you may ask: Show me the meat—how do I get flow? Let's answer this next!

# How to Achieve Flow

Csikszentmihalyi laid out three conditions to achieve flow: (1) your goals must be clear, (2) the feedback mechanism in your environment must be immediate, and (3) there must be a balance between opportunity and capacity.

## Clear Goals

If you're writing code, you must have a clear goal toward which the smaller actions are oriented. In a state of flow, every action naturally leads to the next, which leads to the next, so there must be an end goal. People often reach a state of flow when playing computer games because if you succeed in the small actions—such as jumping over a moving obstacle—you ultimately succeed in the big goal—such as winning the level. To use flow to accelerate your programming productivity, you must have a clear project goal. Every line of code leads you closer to the successful completion of the larger code project. Keeping track of the lines of code you've written is one way to gamify your coding work!

## Feedback Mechanism

A feedback mechanism rewards desired behavior and punishes undesired behavior. Machine learning engineers know that they need to have a great feedback mechanism to train highly effective models. For example, you may teach a robot how to walk by rewarding it for each second it doesn't fall and telling it to optimize for a maximum total reward. The robot can then automatically adjust its action to obtain maximum rewards over time. We humans behave quite similarly when learning new things. We seek appreciation from our parents, teachers, friends, or mentors—even from neighbors we don't like—and adjust our actions to maximize appreciation while minimizing (social) punishments. This way, we learn to take specific actions and avoid others. Receiving feedback is vital for this way of learning.

Feedback is a precondition for flow. To implement more flow in your workday, seek more feedback. Meet weekly with project partners to discuss your code and project goals, then incorporate your partners' feedback.

Publish your code on Reddit or StackOverflow and ask for feedback. Publish your MVP early and often to receive user feedback. Seeking feedback for your programming efforts works like a charm, even if it is delayed gratification, because it'll increase your level of engagement in the activity that led to the feedback. After I published my software application for learning Python, I started to receive a never-ending stream of user feedback, and I was hooked. The feedback kept me going back to work on the code and allowed for many states of flow when I worked on the code to improve the app.

## Balance Opportunity and Capacity

Flow is an active state of mind. If the task is too easy, you get bored and lose the sense of immersion. If it's too hard, you'll throw in the towel early. The task must be challenging but not overwhelming.

Figure 6-1 shows the landscape of possible states of mind; this image is taken and redrawn from Csikszentmihalyi's original research.

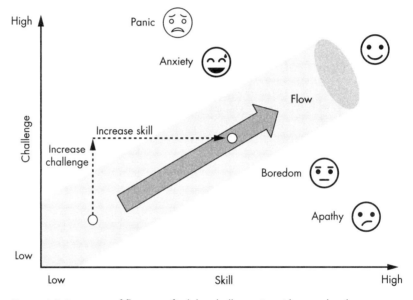

Figure 6-1: In a state of flow, you find the challenge is neither too hard nor too easy, given your current skill level.

The x-axis quantifies your skill level from low to high, and the y-axis quantifies the difficulty of a given task from low to high. So, for example, if the task is much too hard for your skill level, you'll feel panic, and if it's much too easy, you'll feel apathy. But if a task's difficulty matches your current skills, you'll maximize the likelihood of attaining flow.

The trick is to constantly seek harder challenges without reaching anxiety levels and increase your skill level accordingly. This learning loop keeps you in a cycle toward higher and higher productivity and skill, and greater enjoyment of work at the same time.

# Flow Tips for Coders

In his 2015 white paper titled "Crafting Fun User Experiences: A Method to Facilitate Flow," Owen Schaffer identified these seven flow conditions: (1) know what to do, (2) know how to do it, (3) know how well you're doing, (4) know where to go, (5) seek challenges, (6) work on your skills to overcome the high challenges, and (7) free yourself from distractions (Human Factors International). Based on these conditions and my own considerations, I've compiled some quick tips and tactics for attaining flow that are highly biased toward the coding niche.

**Always have a practical code project in the works** rather than spending your time in a state of unfocused learning. You can absorb new information more quickly when it has a real impact on something you care about. I recommend splitting your learning time into 70 percent working on a practical fun project of your choice and 30 percent reading books and tutorials or watching educational courses. I've learned from my personal interaction and correspondence with tens of thousands of coders that a significant portion of coding students have this backward and get stuck in the learning loop, never feeling quite ready to leap into a real project. It's always the same story: these coders remain stuck in programming theory, learning and learning without practical application, making them even more aware of their knowledge limitations—a negative spiral toward paralysis. The way out is to set your clear project goal and push the project through to completion, no matter what. This coincides with one of the three preconditions of flow.

**Work on fun projects that fulfill your purpose.** Flow is a state of excitement, so you must be excited about your work. If you're a professional coder, spend time thinking about the purpose of your work. Find the value of your project. If you're learning to code, lucky you—you can choose a fun project that excites you! Work on projects that are meaningful for you. You'll have more fun, a higher probability of success, and more resilience against temporary setbacks. If you wake up and cannot wait to work on your project, you know that flow is just around the corner.

**Perform from your strengths.** This tip from management consultant Peter Drucker is gold. There will always be more areas in which you are weak than strong. In most activities, your skills are below average. If you focus on your weaknesses, you're virtually guaranteeing failure. Instead, focus on your strengths, build large skill islands around them, and essentially ignore most of your weaknesses. What are you uniquely good at? What are your specific interests in the broad area of computer science? Make lists to answer those questions. One of the activities that will most benefit your progression is figuring out your strengths and then brutally structuring your day around those.

**Block out your coding time in large chunks.** This will give you time to both comprehend the issues and tasks ahead of you—every coder knows that it takes time to load a complicated code project into their head—and get into the rhythm of your tasks. Say Alice and Bob work on a given code project. It takes 20 minutes to attain a state where each completely understands the demands of their code project by glancing over the project, diving into a few code functions, and thinking about the big picture. Alice spends three hours every three days on the project, while Bob spends one hour every day. Who will make more progress in the project? Alice works 53 minutes on the project per day ([3 hours – 20 minutes] / 3). Given the high constant loading time, Bob works only 40 minutes on the project every day. Thus, all other things being equal, Alice will outwork Bob by 13 minutes every day. She has a much higher chance of achieving a state of flow as she can dive deeper into the problem and lose herself entirely in it.

**Eliminate distractions during your flow time.** It seems obvious, but how seldomly it is implemented! Coders who can reduce distractions—social networks, entertainment applications, chitchat about colleagues—attain flow much more often than coders who can't. To reach success, you must do what most others are unwilling to do: shut down distractions. Switch off your smartphone and close that social media tab.

**Do the obvious things you know you need to do**, outside of the task at hand: get plenty of sleep, eat healthily, and get regular exercise. As a coder, you know the expression *garbage-in, garbage-out*: if you feed a system with bad inputs, you'll obtain bad results. Try to cook a tasty meal with decayed food—almost impossible! High-quality input leads to high-quality output.

**Consume high-quality information** because the better your inputs, the better your output. Read programming books instead of shallow blog articles; better yet, read research papers published in top-rated journals, the highest-quality information there is.

## Conclusion

To summarize, here are some of the easiest ways in which you can begin to attempt to attain flow: block large chunks of time, focus on one task, stay healthy and sleep properly, set clear goals, find work you enjoy doing, and actively seek flow.

If you seek flow, you'll eventually find it. If you systematically work in a state of flow daily, you'll boost your work productivity by an order of magnitude. This is a simple yet powerful concept for programmers and other knowledge workers alike. As Mihaly Csikszentmihalyi says:

The best moments in our lives are not the passive, receptive, relaxing times . . . The best moments usually occur if a person's body or mind is stretched to its limits in a voluntary effort to accomplish something difficult and worthwhile.

In the next chapter, you'll dive into the Unix philosophy about *doing one thing well*, a principle that's proven to be not only an excellent way to create a scalable operating system but also a great way to live!

## Resources

Troy Erstling, "The Neurochemistry of Flow States," *Troy Erstling* (blog), *https://troyerstling.com/the-neurochemistry-of-flow-states/*.

Steven Kotler, "How to Get into the Flow State," filmed at A-Fest Jamaica, February 19, 2019, Mindvalley video, *https://youtu.be/XG _hNZ5T4nY/*.

F. Massimini, M. Csikszentmihalyi, and M. Carli, "The Monitoring of Optimal Experience: A Tool for Psychiatric Rehabilitation," *Journal of Nervous and Mental Disease* 175, no. 9 (September 1987).

Kevin Rathunde, "Montessori Education and Optimal Experience: A Framework for New Research," *NAMTA Journal* 26, no. 1 (January 2001): 11–43.

Owen Schaffer, *"Crafting Fun User Experiences: A Method to Facilitate Flow,"* Human Factors International white paper (2015), *https://humanfactors .com/hfi_new/whitepapers/crafting_fun_ux.asp*.

Rony Sklar, "Hyperfocus in Adult ADHD: An EEG Study of the Differences in Cortical Activity in Resting and Arousal States" (MA thesis, University of Johannesburg, 2013), *https://hdl.handle.net/10210/8640*.

# 7

## DO ONE THING WELL
## AND OTHER UNIX PRINCIPLES

*This is the Unix philosophy: Write programs that do one thing
and do it well. Write programs to work together. Write programs to
handle text streams, because that is a universal interface.*
—Douglas McIlroy

 The prevailing philosophy of the Unix
operating system is simple: do one thing
well. This means, for example, that it's generally better to create a function or module
that can solve one problem, reliably and efficiently,
than to try to tackle multiple problems at the same
time. Later in this chapter, you'll see some Python
code examples of "do one thing well" in action and
learn how the Unix philosophy applies to programming. I'll then present
the top principles employed by some of the world's most accomplished
computer engineers in creating today's operating systems. If you're a software engineer, you'll find valuable advice on writing better code in your
own projects.

But first things first: What is Unix anyway, and why should you care?

# The Rise of Unix

Unix is a design philosophy that inspired many of the most popular operating systems today, including Linux and macOS. The family of Unix operating systems emerged in the late 1970s when Bell Systems made the source code of its technology open to the public. Since then, a multitude of extensions and new versions have been developed by universities, individuals, and corporations.

Today, the trademarked Unix standard certifies that operating systems meet specific quality requirements. Unix and Unix-like operating systems have a major impact on computing. About 7 out of 10 web servers run on Linux systems that use Unix as their base. Most supercomputers today run Unix-based systems. Even the macOS is a registered Unix system.

Linus Torvalds, Ken Thompson, Brian Kernighan—the list of Unix developers and maintainers contains the names of some of the world's most impactful coders across the globe. You would think there must be great organizational systems in place to allow programmers all over the world to collaborate to build the massive Unix ecosystem comprising millions of lines of code. And rightly so! The philosophy that enables this scale of collaboration is the acronym DOTADIW (seriously)—or *do one thing and do it well*. Whole books have been written about the Unix philosophy, so here we'll just focus on the most relevant ideas and use Python code snippets to showcase some examples. To the best of my knowledge, no book has ever contextualized the Unix principles for the Python programming language before. So, let's get started!

# Philosophy Overview

The basic idea of the Unix philosophy is to build simple, clear, concise, modular code that is easy to extend and maintain. This can mean many different things—more on this later in the chapter—but the goal is to allow many humans to work together on a codebase by prioritizing readability over efficiency and favoring composability over monolithic design. Monolithic applications are designed without modularity, meaning large parts of the code logic cannot be reused, executed, or debugged without accessing the overall application.

Say you write a program that takes a uniform resource locator (URL) and prints the HTML from this URL on the command line. Let's call this program url_to_html(). According to the Unix philosophy, this program should do one thing well, and that one thing is to take the HTML from the URL and print it to the shell (see Listing 7-1). That's it.

```
import urllib.request


def url_to_html(url):
    html = urllib.request.urlopen(url).read()
    return html
```

*Listing 7-1: A simple code function that reads the HTML from a given URL and returns the string*

That's all you need. Don't add more functionality, such as filtering out tags or fixing bugs. For instance, you might be tempted to add code to fix common mistakes a user might make, like forgetting closing tags, such as a <span> tag that is not closed by </span> as highlighted here:

```
<a href='nostarch.com'><span>Python One-Liners</a>
```

According to the Unix philosophy, even if you spot these types of mistakes, you don't fix them within this specific function.

Another temptation for this simple HTML function is to automatically fix formatting. For example, the following HTML code doesn't look pretty:

```
<a href='nostarch.com'><span>Python One-Liners</span></a>
```

You may prefer this code formatting:

```
<a href='nostarch.com'>
    <span>
        Python One-Liners
    </span>
</a>
```

However, your function's name is url_to_html(), not prettify_html(). Adding a feature such as code prettifying would add a second functionality that may not be needed by some users of the function.

Rather, you'd be encouraged to create another function called prettify _html(url) whose "one thing" is to fix stylistic issues of the HTML. This function may internally use the function url_to_html() to get the HTML before processing it further.

By focusing every function on one purpose only, you improve the maintainability and extensibility of your code. The output of one program is the input of another. You reduce complexity, avoid clutter in the output, and focus on implementing one thing well.

Although a single subprogram may look small, even trivial, you can combine those subprograms to create more complicated programs while keeping them easy to debug.

## 15 Useful Unix Principles

We'll next dive deep into the 15 Unix principles most relevant for today and, where possible, implement them in Python examples. I've compiled these principles from Unix coding experts Eric Raymond and Mike Gancarz and adapted them to modern Python programming. You'll notice that many of these principles comply or overlap with other principles in this book.

### 1. Make Each Function Do One Thing Well

The overarching principle of the Unix philosophy is to *do one thing well.* Let's see what that would look like in code. In Listing 7-2, you implement a function display_html() that takes a URL as a string and displays the pretti-fied HTML on that URL.

```
import urllib.request
import re


def url_to_html(url):
    html = urllib.request.urlopen(url).read()
    return html

def prettify_html(html):
    return re.sub('<\s+', '<', html)

def fix_missing_tags(html):
    if not re.match('<!DOCTYPE html>', html):
        html = '<!DOCTYPE html>\n' + html
    return html

def display_html(url):
    html = url_to_html(url)
    fixed_html = fix_missing_tags(html)
    prettified_html = prettify_html(fixed_html)
    return prettified_html
```

*Listing 7-2: Make each function or program do one thing well.*

This code is depicted in Figure 7-1.

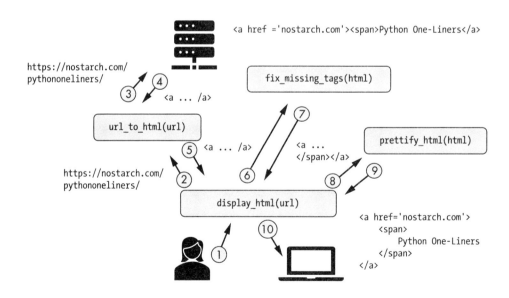

*Figure 7-1: Overview of multiple simple functions—each doing one thing well—working together to accomplish a bigger task*

This code provides a sample implementation that performs the following steps in the function `display_html`:

1. Get the HTML from a given URL location.
2. Fix some missing tags.
3. Prettify the HTML.
4. Return the result to the function caller.

If you run the code with a URL that points to the not-very-pretty HTML code `'<        a href="https://finxter.com">Solve next Puzzle</a>'`, the function `display_html` would fix the poorly formatted (and incorrect) HTML by brokering the inputs and outputs of the small code functions, because each of those does its one thing well.

You would print the result of the main function with this line:

```
print(display_html('https://finxter.com'))
```

This code would print the HTML code to your shell with a new tag and the excess whitespace removed:

```
<!DOCTYPE html>
<a href="https://finxter.com">Solve next Puzzle</a>
```

Think of this whole program as a browser in your terminal. Alice calls the function `display_html(url)`, which takes the URL and passes it to another function `url_to_html(url)`, which collects the HTML from a given URL location. No need to implement the same functionality twice. Fortunately, the coder of the function `url_to_html()` has kept that function minimal so you can use its returned HTML output directly as an input to the function `fix_missing_tags(html)`. In Unix lingo, this is called *piping*: the output of one program is passed as an input to another program. The return value of `fix_missing_tags()` is the fixed HTML code with a closing `</span>` tag that was missing in the original HTML. You then pipe the output into the function `prettify_html(html)` and wait for the result: the corrected HTML with indentation to make it user-friendly. Only then does the function `display_html(url)` return the prettified and fixed HTML code to Alice. You see that a series of small functions connected and piped together can accomplish quite big tasks!

In your project, you could implement another function that doesn't prettify the HTML but only adds the `<!DOCTYPE html>` tag. You could then implement a third function that prettifies the HTML but doesn't add the new tag. By staying small, you can easily create new code based on the existing functionality, and there wouldn't be a lot of redundancy. The modular design of the code enables reusability, maintainability, and extensibility.

Compare this version to a possible monolithic implementation where the function `display_html(url)` would have to do all those small tasks by itself. You couldn't partially reuse functionality, such as retrieving the HTML code from a URL or fixing faulty HTML code. If you use a monolithic code function that does all things itself, it would look like this:

```
def display_html(url):
    html = urllib.request.urlopen(url).read()
    if not re.match('<!DOCTYPE html>', html):
        html = '<!DOCTYPE html>\n' + html
    html = re.sub('<\s+', '<', html)
    return html
```

The function is now more complicated: it handles multiple tasks instead of focusing on one. Even worse, if you implement variants of the same function without removing the whitespace after an opening tag '<', you'd have to copy and paste the remaining code lines. This would lead to code redundancy and reduced readability. The more functionality you add, the worse it will get!

## 2. Simple Is Better Than Complex

*Simple is better than complex* is the foremost principle of this whole book. You've already seen it in many shapes and forms—I stress this point because if you don't take decisive action to simplify, you'll breed complexity. In Python, the principle *simple is better than complex* even made it into the unofficial rule book. If you open a Python shell and enter import this, you obtain the famous *Zen of Python* (see Listing 7-3).

```
> import this
The Zen of Python, by Tim Peters

Beautiful is better than ugly.
Explicit is better than implicit.
Simple is better than complex.
Complex is better than complicated.
Flat is better than nested.
Sparse is better than dense.
Readability counts.
Special cases aren't special enough to break the rules.
Although practicality beats purity.
Errors should never pass silently.
Unless explicitly silenced.
In the face of ambiguity, refuse the temptation to guess.
There should be one-- and preferably only one --obvious way to do it.
Although that way may not be obvious at first unless you're Dutch.
Now is better than never.
Although never is often better than *right* now.
If the implementation is hard to explain, it's a bad idea.
If the implementation is easy to explain, it may be a good idea.
Namespaces are one honking great idea -- let's do more of those!
```

*Listing 7-3: The Zen of Python*

Since we've covered the concept of simplicity at length already, I won't go over it again here. If you're still wondering *why* simple is better than complex, go back to Chapter 1 about the negative productivity effects that originate in high complexity.

## 3. Small Is Beautiful

Rather than writing big code blocks, write small functions and work as an architect brokering the interaction between those functions, as exemplified in Figure 7-1. There are three main reasons to keep your program small:

**Reduce complexity.**

Code is harder to comprehend as it gets longer. This is a cognitive fact: your brain can keep track of only so many chunks of information simultaneously. Too many pieces of information make it hard to see the big picture. By going small and reducing the number of code lines in a function, you *improve readability* and reduce the likelihood of injecting costly bugs into your codebase.

**Improve maintainability.**

Structuring your code in many small pieces of functionality makes it easier to maintain. Adding more small functions is unlikely to incur side effects, whereas in a big, monolithic code block, any changes you make can easily have unintended global effects, especially if multiple programmers are working on the code at the same time.

**Improve testability.**

Many modern software companies use *test-driven development*, which involves using unit tests to stress-test inputs to each function and unit and compare the outputs with the expected ones. This allows you to find and isolate bugs. Unit tests are much more effective and easier to implement in small code, where each function focuses on just one thing, so you know what the expected result should be.

Python itself, rather than an example of small code in Python, is the best example of this principle. Any master coder uses other people's code to improve their coding productivity. Millions of developers have spent countless hours optimizing code that you can import into your code in a split second. Python, like most other programming languages, provides this functionality through libraries. Many of the less frequently used libraries don't ship with the default implementation and need to be explicitly installed. By not providing all the libraries as built-in functionality, the Python installation on your computer remains relatively small but doesn't sacrifice the potential power of external libraries. On top of this, the libraries themselves are relatively small—all of them focus on a restricted subset of functions. Rather than one monolithic library to rule all problems, we have many small libraries, each responsible for a small part of the picture. Small is beautiful.

Every few years, new architectural patterns appear with the promise of breaking up large, monolithic applications into beautiful, small applications to scale up the software development cycle. Recent examples have been the Common Object Request Broker Architecture (CORBA), service-oriented architecture (SOA), and microservices. The idea of these is to break up a large software block into a series of independently deployable components that can then be accessed by multiple programs rather than just one. The hope is to accelerate the overall progress in the software development space by sharing and building upon each other's microservices.

The underlying driver of these trends is the idea of writing modular and reusable code. By studying the ideas presented in this chapter, you've prepared yourself to quickly and fundamentally understand these and upcoming trends with the same direction toward modularity. It pays to stay ahead of the curve by applying sound principles from the start.

**NOTE**    *Diving deeper into this exciting topic is beyond the scope this book, but I suggest you check out an excellent resource on microservices from Martin Fowler at* https://martinfowler .com/articles/microservices.html.

## 4. Build a Prototype as Soon as Possible

The Unix team is a keen proponent of the principle we discussed in Chapter 3, *build an MVP*. This allows you to avoid getting stuck in the cycle of perfectionism, adding more and more features and exponentially increasing complexity without need. If you work on large software applications such as operating systems, you simply cannot afford to go down the route of complexity!

Figure 7-2 shows an example of an early app launch that's stuffed itself full of unnecessary features, in defiance of the MVP principle.

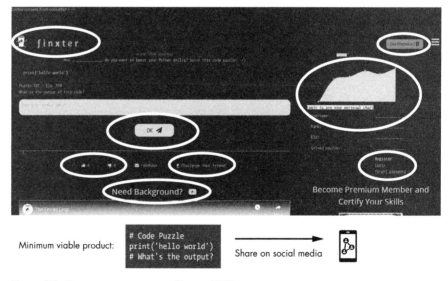

*Figure 7-2: Finxter.com app versus Finxter MVP*

The app has features like interactive solution checking, puzzle voting, user statistics, user management, premium functionality, and related videos along with simple features such as a logo. All of these are unnecessary for an initial launch of the product. In fact, the MVP of the Finxter application should just be an image of a simple code puzzle shared on social media. This is enough to validate the hypothesis of user demand without spending years building the application. *Fail early, fail often, fail forward.*

## 5. Choose Portability Over Efficiency

*Portability* is the ability of a system or a program to be moved from one environment to another and still function properly. One major advantage of software is its portability: you can write a program on your computer, and millions of users can run the same program on their computers without adapting it at all.

However, portability comes at the cost of efficiency. This *portability/ efficiency trade-off* is well documented in technical literature: you can reach higher efficiency by tailoring software to just one type of environment, but this sacrifices portability. *Virtualization* is a great example of this trade-off: by placing an additional layer of software between a piece of software and the underlying infrastructure on which the software runs, your program can run on almost any *physical machine*. Additionally, a virtual machine can carry the current execution state from one physical machine to another. This improves the portability of the software. However, the added layer required for virtualization reduces the runtime and memory efficiency because of the additional overhead of intermediating between the programs and the physical machine.

The Unix philosophy advocates choosing portability over efficiency; this makes sense since the operating system is used by so many.

But the rule of thumb to prefer portability also applies to the broader audience of software developers. Reducing portability means that you reduce your application's value. Today, it is common to improve portability radically—even at the cost of efficiency. Web-based applications are expected to run on every computer with a browser, whether macOS, Windows, or Linux. Web applications are also increasingly accessible, accommodating visual impairment for example, even though hosting a website that facilitates accessibility may be less efficient. Many resources are much more valuable than computing cycles: human lives, human time, and other second-order consequences of computers.

But what does it mean to program for portability, apart from these general considerations? In Listing 7-4 we create a function that computes the average of the specified arguments—the way we've written it, it's not optimized for portability.

```python
import numpy as np

def calculate_average_age(*args):
    a = np.array(args)
    return np.average(a)


print(calculate_average_age(19, 20, 21))
# 20.0
```

*Listing 7-4: Average function, not maximally portable*

This code is not portable for two reasons. First, the function name calculate_average_age() is not general enough to be usable in any other context, despite the fact that it simply calculates an average. You might not think to use it, for example, to calculate the average number of website visitors. Second, it uses a library needlessly because you could easily calculate the average without any external library (see Listing 7-5). It's generally a great idea to use libraries, but only if they add value. In this case, adding a library reduces portability because the user may not have this library installed; plus, it adds little, if any, efficiency.

In Listing 7-5 we recreate the function with superior portability.

```
def average(*args):
    return sum(args) / len(args)


print(average(19, 20, 21))
# 20.0
```

*Listing 7-5: Average function, portable*

We rename the functions to be more general and do away with the unnecessary import. Now you don't have to worry if the library becomes depreciated, and you can port the same code to your other projects.

## 6. Store Data in Flat Text Files

The Unix philosophy encourages the use of *flat text files* for storing data. Flat text files are simple text or binary files without advanced mechanisms to access the file content—unlike many more efficient but also more complicated file formats used by, for example, the database community. These are simple, human-readable data files. The common comma-separated values (CSV) format is an example of a flat file format, where each line relates to one data entry (see Listing 7-6) and someone new to the data can glean some understanding just by looking at it.

```
Property Number,Date,Brand,Model,Color,Stolen,Stolen From,Status,Incident
number,Agency
P13827,01/06/2016,HI POINT,9MM,BLK,Stolen Locally,Vehicle,Recovered
Locally,B16-00694,BPD
P14174,01/15/2016,JENNINGS J22,,COM,Stolen Locally,Residence,Not
Recovered,B16-01892,BPD
P14377,01/24/2016,CENTURY ARMS,M92,,Stolen Locally,Residence,Recovered
Locally,B16-03125,BPD
P14707,02/08/2016,TAURUS,PT740 SLIM,,Stolen Locally,Residence,Not
Recovered,B16-05095,BPD
P15042,02/23/2016,HIGHPOINT,CARBINE,,Stolen Locally,Residence,Recovered
Locally,B16-06990,BPD
P15043,02/23/2016,RUGAR,,,Stolen Locally,Residence,Recovered Locally,B16-
06990,BPD
P15556,03/18/2016,HENRY ARMS,.17 CALIBRE,,Stolen Locally,Residence,Recovered
Locally,B16-08308,BPD
```

*Listing 7-6: Data on stolen guns, from Data.gov, provided as a flat file format (CSV)*

You can share flat text files easily, open them in any text editor, and modify them manually. However, this convenience comes at the cost of efficiency: a data format specialized for a specific purpose could store and read the data much more efficiently. Databases, for example, use their own data files on disk, which use optimizations, like detailed indices and compression schemes to represent dates. If you opened them, you wouldn't understand a thing. These optimizations allow programs to read from the data with less memory consumption and less overhead than general flat text files. In a flat file, a system would have to scan the whole file to read a specific line. Web applications also require a more efficient optimized data representation to allow users quick access with low latency, so they rarely use flat representations and databases.

However, you should use optimized data representations only if you're sure you need them—for example, if you create an application that is highly performance sensitive, such as the Google search engine that can find the web documents most relevant to a given user query in milliseconds! For many smaller applications, such as training a machine learning model from a real-world dataset with 10,000 entries, the CSV format is the recommended way to store the data. Using a database with a specialized format would reduce portability and add unnecessary complexity.

Listing 7-7 gives an example of one situation in which the flat format is preferable. It uses Python, one of the most popular languages for data science and machine learning applications. Here we want to perform a data analysis task on a dataset of images (faces), so we load data from a flat CSV file and process it, favoring the portable approach over the more efficient one of using a database.

```
From sklearn.datasets import fetch_olivetti_faces
From numpy.random import RandomState

rng = RandomState(0)

# Load faces data
faces, _ = fetch_olivetti_faces(...)
```

Listing 7-7: Load data from a flat file for a Python data analysis task

In the function fetch_olivetti_faces, we load scikit-learn's *Olivetti faces* dataset, which contains a set of face images. The loading functions simply read this data and load it into memory before starting with the real computation. No database or hierarchical data structures are needed. The program is self-contained without installing a database or setting up advanced database connections.

NOTE    *I've set up an interactive Jupyter notebook for you to run this example in:* https://blog.finxter.com/clean-code/#Olivetti_Faces/.

## 7. Use Software Leverage to Your Advantage

Using *leverage* means applying a small amount of energy to multiply the effects of your effort. In finance, for example, leverage means to use other people's money to invest and grow. In a large corporation, it might mean using an extensive distributor network to place products in stores worldwide. As a programmer, you should leverage the collective wisdom of generations of coders before you: use libraries for complex functionality rather than coding it from scratch, use StackOverflow and the wisdom of the crowd to fix bugs in your code, or ask other programmers to review your code. These are forms of leverage that allow you to accomplish far more with far less effort.

The second source of leverage comes from computing power. A computer can perform work much faster (and at much lower cost) than a human being. Create better software, share it with more people, employ more computing power, and use other people's libraries and software more often. Good coders create good source code quickly, but great coders tap into the many sources of leverage available to them to elevate their code.

As an example, Listing 7-8 shows a one-liner program from my book *Python One-Liners* (No Starch Press, 2020) that scrapes a given HTML document and finds all occurrences of a URL that contains the substring 'finxter' and either 'test' or 'puzzle'.

```
## Dependencies
import re


## Data
page = '''
<!DOCTYPE html>
<html>
<body>

<h1>My Programming Links</h1>
<a href="https://app.finxter.com/">test your Python skills</a>
<a href="https://blog.finxter.com/recursion/">Learn recursion</a>
<a href="https://nostarch.com/">Great books from NoStarchPress</a>
<a href="http://finxter.com/">Solve more Python puzzles</a>

</body>
</html>
'''


## One-Liner
practice_tests = re.findall("(<a.*?finxter.*?(test|puzzle).*?>)", page)


## Result
print(practice_tests)
# [('<a href="https://app.finxter.com/ ">test your Python skills</a>',
'test'),
#  ('<a href="http://finxter.com/">Solve more Python puzzles</a>', 'puzzle')]
```

*Listing 7-8: One-liner solution to analyze web page links*

By importing the re library, we leverage the powerful technology of regular expressions, instantly putting thousands of lines of code to work and allowing us to write the entire program with a single line. Leverage is a powerful companion on your path to becoming a great coder. For instance, using libraries in your code rather than implementing everything yourself is like using an app to plan your journey rather than working out every detail with a paper map.

**NOTE** *See* https://pythononeliners.com/ *for a video explaining this solution.*

## 8. Avoid Captive User Interfaces

*Captive user interfaces* are those that require the user to interact with the program before proceeding with the main execution flow. Examples are mini-programs such as Secure Shell (SSH), top, cat, and vim, as well as programming language features such as Python's input() function. Captive user interfaces limit the usability of the code because they're designed to run only with human involvement. However, oftentimes the functionality provided by the code behind the captive user interface is also useful for automated programs that must be able to run without manual interaction with users. Roughly speaking, if you put good code behind a captive user interface, it's not reachable without user interaction!

Say you create a simple life expectancy calculator in Python that takes a user's age as input and returns the expected number of years left based on a straightforward heuristic.

"If you're under 85, your life expectancy is 72 minus 80 percent of your age. Otherwise, it's 22 minus 20 percent of your age."

**NOTE** *The heuristic, not the code, is based on a website entry on* Decision Science News.

Your initial Python code might look something like Listing 7-9.

```
def your_life_expectancy():
    age = int(input('how old are you? '))

    if age<85:
        exp_years = 72 - 0.8 * age
    else:
        exp_years = 22 - 0.2 * age

    print(f'People your age have on average {exp_years} years left - use them
wisely!')


your_life_expectancy()
```

*Listing 7-9: Life expectancy calculator—a simple heuristic—implemented as a captive user interface*

Here are some runs of the code in Listing 7-9.

```
> how old are you? 10
People your age have on average 64.0 years left - use them wisely!
> how old are you? 20
```

```
People your age have on average 56.0 years left - use them wisely!
> how old are you? 77
People your age have on average 10.399999999999999 years left - use them
wisely!
```

If you want to try it yourself, I've shared the program in a Jupyter note-book at *https://blog.finxter.com/clean-code/#Life_Expectancy_Calculator/*. But, please, don't take it too seriously!

In Listing 7-9, we used Python's input() function, which blocks pro-gram execution until the user input is received. Without user input, the code doesn't do anything. This captive user interface limits the usability of the code. If you wanted to calculate the life expectancy for every age from 1 to 100 and plot it, you'd have to manually enter 100 different ages and store the results in a separate file. Then, you'd have to copy and paste the results into a new script to plot them. As it is now, the function really does two things: process the user input and calculate the life expectancy, which also violates the first Unix principle: make each function do one thing well.

To make the code compliant with this principle, we'll separate the user interface from the functionality, which is often a great idea to improve your code (see Listing 7-10).

```
# Functionality
def your_life_expectancy(age):
    if age<85:
        return 72 - 0.8 * age
    return 22 - 0.2 * age


# User Interface
age = int(input('how old are you? '))

# Combine user input with functionality and print result
exp_years = your_life_expectancy(age)
print(f'People your age have on average {exp_years} years left - use them
wisely!')
```

*Listing 7-10: Life expectancy calculator—a simple heuristic—without captive user interface*

The code in Listing 7-10 is functionally identical to Listing 7-9, with one significant advantage: we can use this new function in various situations, even those that are unexpected by the initial developer. In Listing 7-11 we use the function to calculate the life expectancy for input ages between 0 and 99 and plot the result; note the portability gained from removing the user input interface.

```
import matplotlib.pyplot as plt


def your_life_expectancy(age):
    '''Returns the expected remaining number of years.'''
    if age<85:
```

```
        return 72 - 0.8 * age
    return 22 - 0.2 * age


# Plot for first 100 years
plt.plot(range(100), [your_life_expectancy(i) for i in range(100)])

# Style plot
plt.xlabel('Age')
plt.ylabel('No. Years Left')
plt.grid()

# Show and save plot
plt.savefig('age_plot.jpg')
plt.savefig('age_plot.pdf')
plt.show()
```

*Listing 7-11: Code to plot the life expectancy for years 0–99*

Figure 7-3 shows the resulting plot.

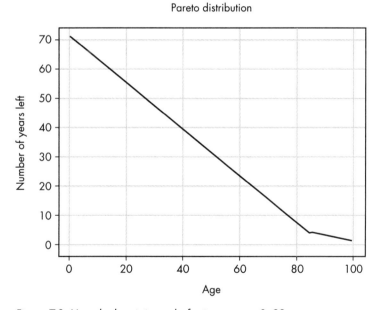

*Figure 7-3: How the heuristic works for input years 0–99*

Okay, any heuristic is crude by design—but the focus here is on how avoiding a captive user interface has helped us put the code to work to produce this plot. If we hadn't adhered to the principle, we couldn't have reused the original code function your_life_expectancy because the captive user interface required a user input for each year 0 to 99. By considering the principle, we've simplified the code and opened up all kinds of future programs to use and build upon the heuristic. Instead of optimizing for one specific use case, we've written the code in a general way that can be used by hundreds of different applications. Why not create a library out of it?

## 9. Make Every Program a Filter

There's a good argument to be made that every program already is a filter. A filter transforms an input to an output using a specific filtering mechanism. This allows us to easily string together multiple programs by using the output of one as the input of another, thereby increasing the reusability of your code significantly. For example, it's generally not a good practice to print the result of a computation in the function itself—instead, the philosophy suggests that the program should return a string that can then be printed, written into a file, or used as input for another program.

For example, a program that sorts a list can be considered a filter that filters the unsorted elements into a sorted order, as in Listing 7-12.

```
def insert_sort(lst):

    # Check if the list is empty
    if not lst:
        return []

    # Start with sorted 1-element list
    new = [lst[0]]

    # Insert each remaining element
    for x in lst[1:]:
        i = 0
        while i<len(new) and x>new[i]:
            i = i + 1
        new.insert(i, x)

    return new


print(insert_sort([42, 11, 44, 33, 1]))
print(insert_sort([0, 0, 0, 1]))
print(insert_sort([4, 3, 2, 1]))
```

Listing 7-12: This insertion sort algorithm filters an unsorted list to a sorted list.

The algorithm creates a new list and inserts each element at the position where all elements on the left are smaller than the inserted element. The function uses a complex filter to change the order of the elements, transforming the input list into a sorted output list.

If any program already is a filter, you should design it as such by using intuitive input/output mapping. Let me explain this next.

The gold standard for filters is a *homogeneous* input/output mapping where one type of input is mapped to the same type of output. For example, if someone talks to you in English, they expect you to respond in English—and not in another language. Similarly, if a function takes an input argument, the expected output is a function return value. If a program reads from a file, the expected output is a file. If a program reads the input from the standard input, it should write the program to the standard output. You get the point: the most intuitive way to design a filter is to keep the data in the same category.

Listing 7-13 shows a negative example with *heterogeneous* input/output mapping where we build an `average()` function that transforms the input arguments into their average—but instead of returning the average value, `average()` prints the result to the shell.

```
def average(*args):
    print(sum(args)/len(args))


average(1, 2, 3)
# 2.0
```

*Listing 7-13: Negative example of heterogeneous input/output mapping*

A better approach, shown in Listing 7-14, makes the function `average()` return the average value (homogeneous input/output mapping), which you can then print to the standard output in a separate function call using the `print()` function. This is better because it allows you, for example, to write the output into a file rather than print it—or even use it as an input for another function.

```
def average(*args):
    return sum(args)/len(args)


avg = average(1, 2, 3)
print(avg)
# 2.0
```

*Listing 7-14: Positive example of homogeneous input/output mapping*

Sure, some programs filter from one category to another—for example, writing a file to the standard output or translating English to Spanish. But following the principle of creating programs that do one thing well (see Unix Principle 1), these programs should do nothing else. This is the gold standard of writing intuitive and natural programs—design them as filters!

## 10. Worse Is Better

This principle suggests that developing code with less functionality is often the better approach in practice. When resources are limited, it's better to release a worse product and be first on the market than strive continually to make it better before you can release it. This principle, conceived by list processing (LISP) developer Richard Gabriel in the late eighties, is similar to the MVP principle from Chapter 3. Don't take this counterintuitive principle too literally. Worse is not better from a qualitative perspective. If you had infinite time and resources, it would be best always to make the program perfect. However, in a world with limited resources, releasing something worse is often more efficient. For instance, a crude and straightforward solution to a problem gives you a first-mover advantage, attracts quick feedback from the early adopters, and gains momentum and attention early in the software development process. Many practitioners argue that a second-mover must invest far more energy and resources to create a far superior product that's able to pull users away from the first-mover.

## 11. Clean Code Is Better Than Clever Code

I slightly modified the original principle in the Unix philosophy, *clarity is better than cleverness*, first to focus the principle on programming code and, second, to align it with the principles you've already learned: how to *write clean code* (see Chapter 4).

This principle highlights the trade-off between clean and clever code: clever code shouldn't come at the cost of simplicity.

For example, have a look at the simple bubble sort algorithm in Listing 7-15. A bubble sort algorithm sorts a list by going through it iteratively and switching the position of any two adjacent elements that aren't sorted: the smaller element goes to the left, and the larger element goes to the right. Each time that happens, the list becomes a bit more sorted.

```python
def bubblesort(l):
    for boundary in range(len(l)-1, 0, -1):
        for i in range(boundary):
            if l[i] > l[i+1]:
                l[i], l[i+1] = l[i+1], l[i]
    return l

l = [5, 3, 4, 1, 2, 0]
print(bubblesort(l))
# [0, 1, 2, 3, 4, 5]
```

*Listing 7-15: Bubble sort algorithm in Python*

The algorithm in Listing 7-15 is readable and clear, and it achieves the goal and doesn't contain unnecessary code.

Now, suppose your bright colleague argues that you could shorten the code using *conditional assignments* to express the if statement with one less line of code (see Listing 7-16).

```python
def bubblesort_clever(l):
    for boundary in range(len(l)-1, 0, -1):
        for i in range(boundary):
            l[i], l[i+1] = (l[i+1], l[i]) if l[i] > l[i+1] else (l[i], l[i+1])
    return l

print(bubblesort_clever(l))
# [0, 1, 2, 3, 4, 5]
```

*Listing 7-16: "Clever" bubble sort algorithm in Python*

The trick doesn't improve the code but does reduce readability and clarity. Conditional assignment features may be clever, but using them comes at the cost of expressing your ideas with clean code. For more tips on how to write clean code, please refer to Chapter 4.

## 12. Design Programs to Connect With Other Programs

Your programs do not live in isolation. A program is called to perform a task, either by a human being or by another program. You therefore need to design the API to work with the outside world—users or other programs. By adhering to Unix Principle 9, *make any program a filter*, which says to ensure the input/output mapping is intuitive, you're already designing connected programs rather than making them live in isolation. The great programmer is as much an architect as a craftsperson. They create new programs as a unique combination of old and new functions and other people's programs. As a result, interfaces are able to be front and center of the development cycle.

## 13. Make Your Code Robust

A codebase is *robust* if it cannot be easily broken. There are two perspectives on code robustness: the programmer's view and the user's view.

As the programmer, you could potentially break code by modifying it. A codebase is therefore *robust against change* if even a careless programmer can work on the codebase without being able to destroy its functionality easily. Say you have a big, monolithic code block and every programmer in your organization has *edit access* to that whole thing. Any small change could break the whole thing. Now, compare this to code developed by organizations like Netflix or Google, where every change has to go through multiple approval levels before being deployed in the real world; changes are thoroughly tested, so deployed code is protected against breaking changes. By adding layers of protection, Google and Netflix have made their code more robust than a fragile, monolithic codebase.

One way to accomplish codebase robustness is to control access rights so that individual developers are not able to damage the application without verifying with at least one additional person that the change is more likely to add value than damage the code. The process may come at a price of less agility, but the price is worth paying if you're not a one-person startup. We've already seen other ways to ensure code robustness throughout the book: small is beautiful, create functions that do one thing well, use test-driven development, keep things simple. A few other easily applied techniques are the following:

- Use versioning systems such as Git so that you can recover previous versions of your code.
- Back up your application data regularly to make it recoverable (data is not part of a versioning system).

- Use distributed systems to avoid a single point of failure: run your application on multiple machines to reduce the probability of a failing machine adversely affecting your application. Say one machine has a failure probability of 1 percent per day—it'll fail about every 100 days. Creating a distributed system of five machines that fail independently can theoretically reduce your failure probability to $0.01^5 \times 100\% = 0.00000001\%$.

For a user, an application is robust if you cannot easily break it by providing faulty or even malicious inputs. Assume that your users will behave like a mob of gorillas smacking the keyboard and submitting random series of characters and that highly skilled hackers understand the application better than you and are ready to exploit even the smallest security issue. Your application must be robust against both types of users.

It's relatively simple to shield against the former group. Unit testing is one powerful tool: test any function against any function input you can think of, especially border cases. For example, if your function takes an integer and calculates the square root, check that it can handle negative inputs and 0 because unhandled exceptions would break the chain of reliable, simple, chainable programs. However, unhandled exceptions lead to another more subtle problem that was brought to my attention by security expert and technical editor of this book, Noah Spahn: providing input to break a program can give attackers a foothold into the host operating system. So, check your program's ability to process all kinds of inputs and, thereby, make your code more robust!

### 14. Repair What You Can—But Fail Early and Noisily

While you should repair problems in your code wherever possible, you shouldn't hide the errors you cannot fix. A hidden error will quickly compound, becoming bigger and bigger the longer it remains hidden.

Errors can accumulate. For example, say the speech recognition system in your driving assistance app is fed faulty training data classifying two completely different phonetic waves as the same word (see Figure 7-4). So your code raises an error trying to map two completely different phonetic waves to the same English word (for example, the error may occur as you try to store this contradictory information in an inverted index that maps English terms to phonetic waves). You can write your code in two ways: hide the error or propagate the error up to the application, user, or programmer. While many coders intuitively want to hide errors from the users to improve usability, this is not the most sensible approach. Error messages should carry useful information. If your code makes you aware of this problem early, you could figure out a solution in advance. You better become aware of errors early before their consequences cumulate and destroy millions of dollars or even human lives.

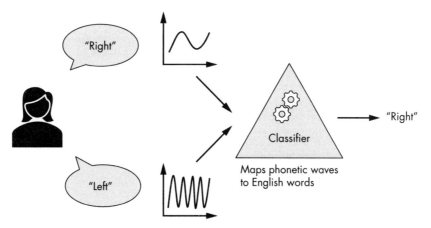

Figure 7-4: Classifier in the training phase maps two different phonetic waves to the same English word.

It's better to raise unfixable errors and hand them to the user than bury them, even if the user doesn't appreciate the error message and the usability of your application decreases. The alternative is to bury the errors until they have grown too big to ever handle.

To continue with our faulty training data example, Listing 7-17 shows an example in which the Python classify() function takes one input argument—the wave to be classified—and returns the English word associated with this classification. Say you've implemented a duplicate_check(wave, word) function that checks whether a substantially different wave in your database results in the same classification using the wave and word pairs. In this case, the classification is ambiguous because two completely different waves map to the same English word, and you should share this with the user by raising a ClassificationError rather than returning a random guess of the classified word. Yes, the user will be annoyed, but at least they have a chance to handle the consequences of the error themselves. *Repair what you can—but fail early and noisily!*

```python
def classify(wave):
    # Do the classification
    word = wave_to_word(wave)      # to be implemented

    # Check if another wave
    # results in the same word
    if duplicate_check(wave, word):

        # Do not return a random guess
        # and hide the error!
        raise ClassificationError('Not Understood')

    return word
```

Listing 7-17: Code snippet with noisy failure instead of random guess if the wave cannot be classified unambiguously

### 15. Avoid Hand-Hacking: Write Programs to Write Programs If You Can

The principle suggests that code that can be generated automatically *should be*, because humans are notoriously prone to failures, especially in an activity that's repetitive and boring. There are many ways to accomplish this—in fact, modern high-level programming languages such as Python are compiled down to machine code using such programs. By writing programs to write programs, the creators of those compilers helped high-level programmers to create all kinds of application software without needing to worry about low-level hardware programming languages. Without those programs writing programs for us, the computer industry would still be in its infancy.

Code generators and compilers already produce large amounts of source code today. Let's examine an additional way to think of this principle. Today, the technologies of machine learning and artificial intelligence lift this concept of writing programs to write programs to yet another level. Intelligent machines (machine learning models) are assembled by humans and then go on to rewrite (and tune) themselves based on data. Technically, a machine learning model is a program that has rewritten itself many times over until its behavior has maximized a set fitness function (usually set by humans). As machine learning permeates (and prevails over) more areas of computer science, this principle will become more and more relevant in modern computing. Human programmers will still play a major role in using those powerful tools; after all, compilers have not replaced human labor but have instead opened up a new world of applications created by human programmers. I expect that the same will happen in programming: machine learning engineers and software architects will design advanced applications by connecting the different low-level programs, such as machine learning models. Well, that's one view on the topic—yours may be more or less optimistic!

## Conclusion

In this chapter, you've learned 15 principles designed by the Unix creators to write better code. It's worth repeating them—as you read through the list, think about how each principle applies to your current code project.

- Make each function do one thing well.
- Simple is better than complex.
- Small is beautiful.
- Build a prototype as soon as possible.
- Choose portability over efficiency.
- Store data in flat text files.
- Use software leverage to your advantage.

- Avoid captive user interfaces.
- Make every program a filter.
- Worse is better.
- Clean code is better than clever code.
- Design programs to be connected with other programs.
- Make your code robust.
- Repair what you can—but fail early and noisily.
- Write programs to write programs.

In the next chapter, you'll learn about the impact of minimalism on design and how it can help you design applications that delight your users by doing less.

## Resources

Mike Gancarz, *The Unix Philosophy*, Boston: Digital Press, 1994.

Eric Raymond, *The Art of Unix*, Boston: Addison-Wesley, 2004, *http://www.catb.org/~esr/writings/taoup/html/*.

# 8

## LESS IS MORE IN DESIGN

Simplicity is a way of life for coders. While you may not see yourself as a designer, chances are that you will create many user interfaces in your coding career. Whether you need to create a visually appealing dashboard as a data scientist, an easy-to-use API as a database engineer, or a simple web frontend to fill data into a smart contract as a blockchain developer, knowing basic design principles will save the day for you and your team—and they're easy to grasp, too! The design principles covered in this chapter are universal.

Specifically, you'll explore one vital area in computer science that benefits most from a minimalistic mindset: design and user experience (UX). To get an idea of the importance of minimalism in design and UX, think of the differences between Yahoo Search and Google Search, the Blackberry and the iPhone, Facebook Dating and Tinder: the winning technologies often come with a radically simple user interface. Could it be that *less is more* in design?

We'll first take a brief tour of some creations that have benefited from the radical focus of their creators. Later, we'll see how you can apply minimalism in your own design efforts.

## Minimalism in the Evolution of Mobile Phones

A prime example of minimalism in computing design can be seen in the evolution of mobile phones (see Figure 8-1). The Nokia Mobira Senator, one of the earliest commercial "mobile" phones, was released in the 1980s, weighed 10 kg, and was quite complicated to handle. A year later, Motorola marketed its own DynaTAC 8000X model that was 10 times lighter—weighing only 1 kg. Nokia had to up its game. In 1992, Nokia came up with the 1011 at half the weight of the DynaTAC 8000X. Nearly a decade later in 2000, in accordance with Moore's laws, Nokia achieved mega-success with its iconic Nokia 3310, weighing only 88 g. As mobile phone technology grew more sophisticated and complex, the user interface, including the size, weight, and even number of buttons, became drastically less complex. The evolution of mobile phones proves that radically minimalistic design can be done, even as the complexity of the applications increases by orders of magnitude. You could even argue that minimalistic design has paved the way for the success of smartphone apps and their exploding usage in today's world. You'd have a hard time browsing the web, using mapping services, or sending video messages with the Nokia Senator!

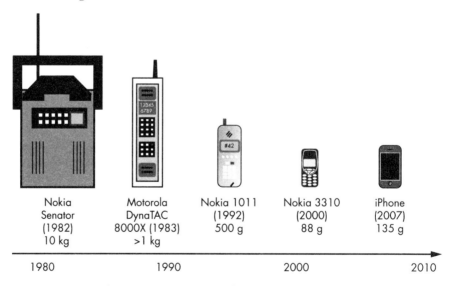

*Figure 8-1: Some milestones in the evolution of mobile phones*

Minimalistic design is apparent in many products besides smartphones. Companies use it to improve UX and create focused applications. What better example could there be than the Google search engine?

## Minimalism in Search

In Figure 8-2, I've sketched a minimalistic design that resembles how Google—and its copycats—designs its primary user interface as a radically simplified gate into the web. Make no mistake, the minimalistic and clean design is not an accident. This landing page is frequented by billions of users every day. It may be *the* primary real estate on the web. A small advertisement on the Google landing page could generate billions of clicks and, likely, billions of USD in revenue for Google, but Google hasn't allowed these ads to clutter its landing page, despite the loss of short-term revenue opportunity—the company managers know that maintaining brand integrity and focus, expressed through minimalistic design, is even more valuable than the revenues that could be generated through selling this prime real estate.

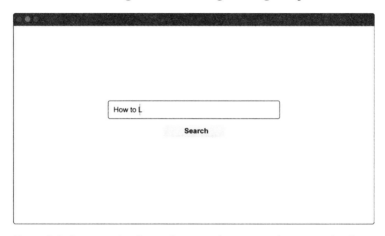

*Figure 8-2: An example of a modern search engine with a minimalist design*

Now compare this clean, focused design to the kind that alternative search engines like Bing and Yahoo! use to exploit their primary real estate (see Figure 8-3).

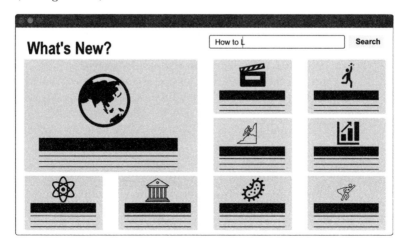

*Figure 8-3: Search engine or news aggregator?*

Even for basic search engine sites, companies like Yahoo! have followed the same path: they cluttered their valuable real estate with news and advertisements to boost short-term revenues. But these revenues didn't last because the design drove away the commodity that generated it: users. Reduced usability led to a competitive disadvantage and ongoing erosion of users' habitual search behavior. Any additional website element unrelated to search increases the cognitive challenge to the user, who must ignore attention-grabbing headlines, ads, and images. The smooth search experience is one of the reasons why Google continuously increased its market share. The last word isn't spoken yet, but the rising popularity of focused search engines during the last decades indicates the superiority of minimalistic and focused design.

## Material Design

Google developed and currently adheres to the *Material Design* philosophy and design language, which describes a way to organize and design screen elements according to what users already understand intuitively: physical world elements such as paper, cards, pens, and shadow. Figure 8-3 from the previous section shows such an example of material design. The website is structured into cards, each card representing a piece of content, which creates a layout that resembles a newspaper with an image and some headline text. The look and feel of the website are almost materialistic, even though the three-dimensional (3D) effect is a pure illusion on the two-dimensional (2D) screen.

Figure 8-4 compares a material design on the left and a non-material design with unnecessary elements stripped out on the right. You could argue that the non-material design is more minimalistic, and, in a way, you would be right. It takes less space and uses fewer colors and fewer nonfunctional visual elements like shadows. However, lacking boundaries and an intuitively familiar layout, the non-material design is often more confusing to the reader. The true minimalist will always use fewer costly resources to accomplish the same task. In some cases, this means reducing the number of visual elements on a website. In other cases, this means adding some elements to reduce the time the user has to think. As a rule of thumb: user time is a much scarcer resource than screen space.

You can find a full introduction to material design with many beautiful case studies at *https://material.io/design/*. New design systems will emerge and users will get more and more used to digital work, so the material metaphors may well become less useful for the next generation of computer users. For now, just note that minimalism requires careful consideration of the relevant resources: time, space, and money—and you must weigh them according to the needs of your application. To sum up, minimalistic design gets rid of all unnecessary elements and results in a beautiful product likely to delight your users.

Next, you'll learn how to achieve it.

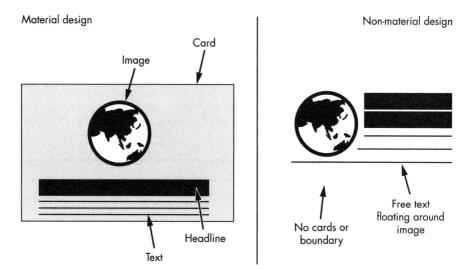

Figure 8-4: Material versus "non-material" design

## How to Achieve Minimalistic Design

In this section, you'll learn some technical tips and methods for how to achieve a focused, minimalistic design.

### Use Whitespace

Whitespace is one of the key pillars of minimalistic design. Adding whitespace to your application may seem like a waste of valuable real estate. You must be crazy not to use every inch of a highly-trafficked website, right? You could use it for advertisements, "call to actions" to sell more products, additional information about the value proposition, or more personalized recommendations. The more successful your app becomes, the more stakeholders will fight for every bit of attention they can get, and it's likely that nobody will ask you to remove non-whitespace elements from your app.

Thinking "subtractively" may not come naturally; however, replacing design elements with whitespace will improve clarity and result in a more focused UX. Successful companies manage to keep the main thing the main thing by using whitespace to remain focused and sharp. For example, Google's landing page uses a lot of whitespace, and Apple uses lots of whitespace when presenting its products. When thinking about your users, remember this: if you confuse them, you'll lose them. Whitespace increases the clarity of user interfaces.

Figure 8-5 shows a simple design idea for an online pizza delivery service. The whitespace supports the focus on the main thing: getting customers to order pizza. Unfortunately, seldom will a pizza delivery service be bold enough to use whitespace in such an extreme way.

*Figure 8-5: Use lots of whitespace*

Whitespace can improve the clarity of text, too. Have a look at Figure 8-6, which compares two ways of formatting a paragraph.

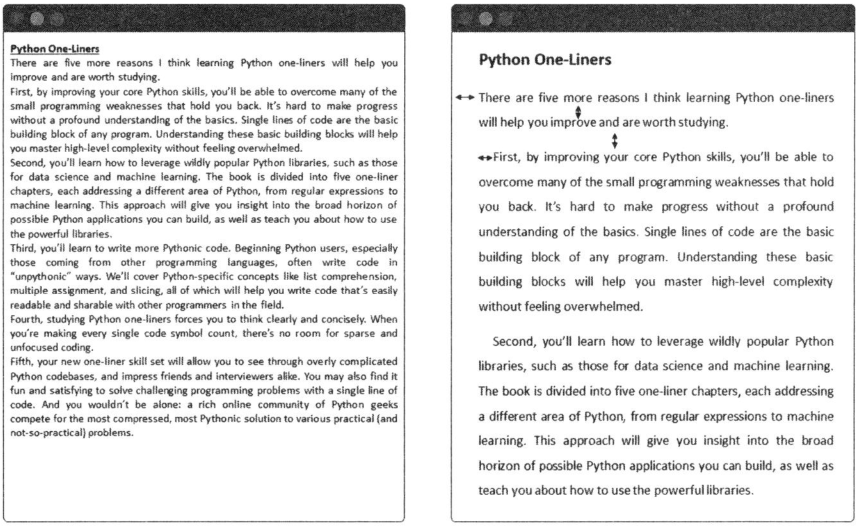

**Python One-Liners**
There are five more reasons I think learning Python one-liners will help you improve and are worth studying.
First, by improving your core Python skills, you'll be able to overcome many of the small programming weaknesses that hold you back. It's hard to make progress without a profound understanding of the basics. Single lines of code are the basic building block of any program. Understanding these basic building blocks will help you master high-level complexity without feeling overwhelmed.
Second, you'll learn how to leverage wildly popular Python libraries, such as those for data science and machine learning. The book is divided into five one-liner chapters, each addressing a different area of Python, from regular expressions to machine learning. This approach will give you insight into the broad horizon of possible Python applications you can build, as well as teach you about how to use the powerful libraries.
Third, you'll learn how to write more Pythonic code. Beginning Python users, especially those coming from other programming languages, often write code in "unpythonic" ways. We'll cover Python-specific concepts like list comprehension, multiple assignment, and slicing, all of which will help you write code that's easily readable and sharable with other programmers in the field.
Fourth, studying Python one-liners forces you to think clearly and concisely. When you're making every single code symbol count, there's no room for sparse and unfocused coding.
Fifth, your new one-liner skill set will allow you to see through overly complicated Python codebases, and impress friends and interviewers alike. You may also find it fun and satisfying to solve challenging programming problems with a single line of code. And you wouldn't be alone: a rich online community of Python geeks compete for the most compressed, most Pythonic solution to various practical (and not-so-practical) problems.

**Python One-Liners**

There are five more reasons I think learning Python one-liners will help you improve and are worth studying.

First, by improving your core Python skills, you'll be able to overcome many of the small programming weaknesses that hold you back. It's hard to make progress without a profound understanding of the basics. Single lines of code are the basic building block of any program. Understanding these basic building blocks will help you master high-level complexity without feeling overwhelmed.

Second, you'll learn how to leverage wildly popular Python libraries, such as those for data science and machine learning. The book is divided into five one-liner chapters, each addressing a different area of Python, from regular expressions to machine learning. This approach will give you insight into the broad horizon of possible Python applications you can build, as well as teach you about how to use the powerful libraries.

*Figure 8-6: Whitespace in text*

The left side of Figure 8-6 is far less readable. The right side injects whitespace to improve readability and UX: margins on the left and right around the text block, indentation of paragraphs, an increased line height, top and bottom margins around paragraphs, and increased font size. The costs of this additional space are negligible: scrolling is cheap, and we don't have to physically cut more trees for paper when the publication is digital. On the other hand, the benefits are very real: the UX of your website or application improves significantly!

## Remove Design Elements

The principle is simple: go over each design element, one by one, and throw it out if possible. *Design elements* are any visible elements of the user interface, such as menu items, calls to action, featured lists, buttons, images, boxes, shadows, form fields, pop-ups, videos, and everything else that takes up real estate in your user interface. Literally, go over all design elements and ask: *Can I remove it?* You'll be surprised how often the answer will be *yes!*

Make no mistake—removing design elements is not easy! You've spent time and effort creating them, and the sunk cost bias makes you tempted to hold on to your creations even when they're unnecessary. Figure 8-7 shows an idealized editing process in which you classify each element according to its importance regarding the UX. For example, does a menu item referring to your company's blog help the user in the checkout process when ordering a product? No, so it should be classified as not important. Amazon has stripped all unnecessary design elements from the ordering process, for instance, by introducing the one-click buy button. When I first learned about this method in a scientific writing workshop, it completely transformed the way I thought about editing. Removing unimportant and less important design elements guarantees improved usability with little risk. But only truly great designers have the boldness to remove *important* design elements and leave only *very important* elements. Yet, this is what separates great from merely good design.

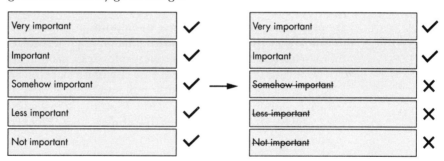

Figure 8-7: Idealized editing process

Figure 8-8 shows an example of a cluttered design and a minimalistic, edited design. The order page on the left is what you may well see from an online pizza delivery service. Some elements are very important, such as the address to which to deliver the pizza and the order button, but those like the overly detailed ingredient list and "What's New?" info box are less so. On the right, you see an edited version of this order page. We removed unnecessary elements, focused on the most popular upsells, combined the ingredients list with the headline, and combined the labels with the form elements. This allowed us to add more whitespace and even increase the size of a very important design element: the image of the tasty pizza! The reduced clutter and increased focus are likely to increase the conversion rate of the order page through an improved UX.

Figure 8-8: Remove unimportant elements: unfocused order page with many design elements (left); focused order page with unnecessary design elements removed (right).

## Remove Features

The best way to implement a minimalistic design is to remove whole features from your application! You've already studied this idea in Chapter 3 about creating MVPs, which have the minimum number of features needed to validate a hypothesis. Minimizing the number of features is equally helpful in helping an established business refocus its product offerings.

Over time, applications tend to accumulate features—a phenomenon known as *feature creep*. As a result, more and more focus must be shifted toward maintaining existing features. Feature creep leads to bloated software, and bloated software leads to technical debt. This reduces the agility of an organization. The idea behind removing features is to release energy, time, and resources and to reinvest into the few features that matter most to your users.

Popular examples of feature creep and its harmful effects on usability are Yahoo!, AOL, and MySpace, who all somehow lost their focused products by adding too much stuff to the user interfaces.

In contrast, the most successful products in the world are focused and have resisted feature creep, even if it doesn't look like it. Microsoft is a great example of how building *focused products* helped it become a super successful company. A common perception is that Microsoft products such as Windows are slow, inefficient, and loaded with too many features. But nothing could be further from the truth! *What you see is all there is*—you don't *see* the myriads of features Microsoft has removed. Although Microsoft is huge, it's actually very focused considering its size. Hundreds of thousands of software developers write new Microsoft code every day. Here's what Eric Traut, a famous engineer who's worked for both Apple and Microsoft, has to say about Microsoft's focused approach to software engineering:

A lot of people think of Windows as this really large, bloated operating system, and that may be a fair characterization, I have to admit. It is large. It contains a lot of stuff in it. But at its core, the kernel and the components that make up the very core of the operating system actually is pretty streamlined.

To sum this up, when creating an application used by many users for a long period, removing features must be a core activity of your daily effort because it frees up resources, time, energy, and user interface space that can be reinvested into improving features that matter.

### Reduce Variations of Fonts and Colors

Extensive variability leads to complexity. If you vary the font types, font sizes, and colors too much, you'll increase cognitive friction, increase the perceived complexity of the user interface, and sacrifice clarity. As a minimalistic coder, you don't want to build these psychological effects into your application. Effective minimalist design often focuses on only one or two font types, one or two colors, and one or two font sizes. Figure 8-9 exemplifies the consistent and minimalistic use of font types, sizes, colors, and contrasts. That said, do note that there are many approaches to design and many ways to accomplish focus and minimalism on all levels. A minimalistic design might, for instance, use many different colors to make the playful, colorful attributes of an application stand out.

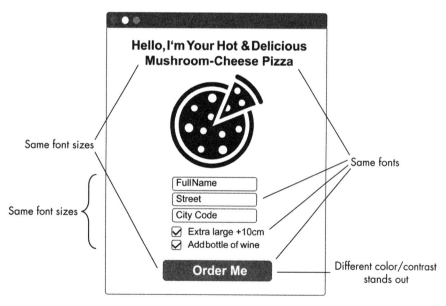

Figure 8-9: Minimalistic use of font sizes, font types, colors, and contrasts

### Be Consistent

An application doesn't normally consist of a single user interface but a series of interfaces handling the user interaction. This leads us to another dimension of minimalistic design: *consistency*. We define consistency as the degree to which we've minimized the variability of design choices in a given app. Instead of presenting the user a different "look and feel" in each step in the interaction, consistency ensures that the application feels like a coherent whole. For example, Apple provides many iPhone apps, such as browsers, health apps, and mapping services, and all have a similar look and feel and are recognizable as Apple products. It can be challenging to get different app developers to agree on a consistent design, but it's extremely important for the strength of the Apple brand. To ensure brand consistency, software companies use *brand guidelines* that any contributing developer must adhere to. Make sure to check off this box when creating your own application. You might accomplish this with the consistent use of templates and (CSS) stylesheets.

## Conclusion

This chapter focused on how minimalistic designers have come to dominate the world of design, as exemplified by some of the most successful software companies such as Apple and Google. More often than not, the leading technologies and user interfaces are radically simple. Nobody knows what the future holds, but it seems that the wide adoption of speech recognition and virtual reality will result in even simpler user interfaces. The ultimate minimalistic design is invisible. With ubiquitous computing on the rise—for example, Alexa and Siri—I think we'll see even simpler and even more focused user interfaces in the decades ahead. So, to answer the question posed in the beginning: *yes, less is more in design!*

In the next and final chapter of this book, we'll conclude by discussing focus—and its relevance for today's programmers.

## Resources

Apple's documentation of human interface design: *https://developer.apple.com/design/human-interface-guidelines/*

Documentation for the material design style: *https://material.io/design/introduction/*

# 9

## FOCUS

In this short chapter, you'll take a quick tour through the most important lesson in this book: how to focus. We started this book with a discussion of complexity, the origin of many productivity obstacles. Here, we summarize how to tackle complexity based on what you've learned in this book.

### The Weapon Against Complexity

The main thesis of this book is that complexity leads to chaos. Chaos is the flip side of focus. To solve the challenges posed by complexity, you need to use the powerful weapon of *focus*.

To justify this argument, let's look at the scientific concept of *entropy*, well known in many scientific fields such as thermodynamics and information theory. Entropy defines the degree of randomness, disorder, and uncertainty in a system. High entropy means high randomness and chaos. Low entropy means order and predictability. Entropy is at the heart of the famous second law of thermodynamics that states that *the entropy of a system increases with time—resulting in a state of high entropy.*

Figure 9-1 depicts entropy through the example of an arrangement of a fixed number of particles. On the left, you see a state with low entropy where the structure of the particles resembles a house. The location of each particle is predictable and follows a higher-level order and structure. There's a greater plan for how the particles must be arranged. On the right, you see a state with high entropy: the house structure has broken down. The pattern of particles has lost its order, giving way to chaos. Over time—if no external force exerts energy to reduce entropy—entropy will increase, and all order will be destroyed. Ruined castles, for example, are a testament to the second law of thermodynamics. You may ask: What does thermodynamics have to do with coding productivity? It'll become clear in a moment. Let's keep thinking from first principles.

Low entropy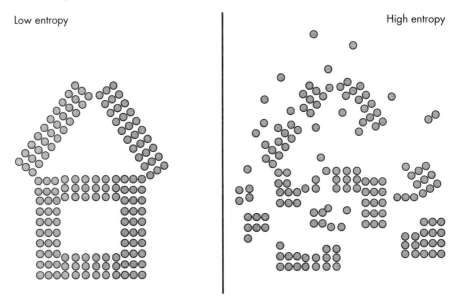High entropy

*Figure 9-1: Contrasting states of low and high entropy*

Productivity means creating something, whether you're building a house, writing a book, or writing a software app. Essentially, to be productive, you must *reduce entropy* so that resources are arranged in a way to make your greater plan whole.

Figure 9-2 shows the relationship between entropy and productivity. You are a creator and a builder. You take raw resources and move them from a state of high entropy into a state of low entropy using focused effort toward the attainment of a greater plan. That's it! This is the secret and everything you need in life to be super productive and successful: take time to carefully *plan* your course of action, set specific goals, and design regular habits and action steps that will give you the result you want. Then apply *focused effort* using all resources you possess—time, energy, money, and people—until your plan comes true.

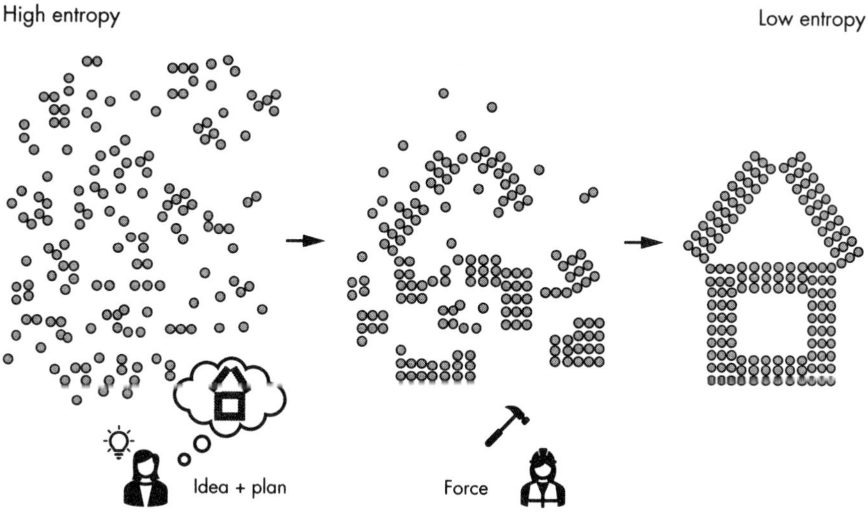

High entropy                                                Low entropy

Idea + plan                    Force

Figure 9-2: Relationship between entropy and productivity

It may sound trivial, but most people do this wrong. They may never apply this focused effort toward an idea's attainment, so the idea remains trapped in their heads. Others may live from day to day, never planning anything new. Only if you do both—plan carefully and focus your effort—will you become a productive person. So, to become a builder of, say, a smartphone app, you must bring order to the chaos by planning and by applying focused effort until you achieve your goal.

If it is that simple, why isn't everyone doing it? The primary obstacle, as you've guessed, is the complexity that often comes from a lack of focus. If you have multiple plans or you allow your plans to change more than necessary over time, you're more likely to move just a few steps toward your goal before aborting the whole thing. Only if you focus for a long enough time on *one* plan can you actually accomplish it. This holds for small accomplishments, such as reading a book (you almost have this done!), and big accomplishments, such as writing and publishing your first app. Focus is the missing link.

Figure 9-3 is a graphic explaining the power of focus, plain and simple.

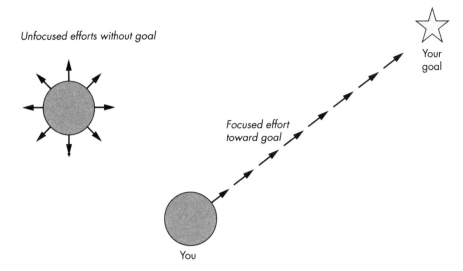

Figure 9-3: Same effort, different result

You have limited time and energy. Say you've got eight hours of full-on effort in a given day. You can decide how to spend those units. Most people spend a little time on a lot of activities. For example, Bob may spend one hour in meetings, one hour coding, one hour browsing social media, one hour in project discussions, one hour chitchatting, one hour editing code documentation, one hour thinking about a new project, and one hour writing a novel. Bob is likely to achieve average results at best in all the activities he does because he spends so little time and effort on each of them. Alice may spend eight hours doing one thing: coding. She does it every day. She makes rapid progress toward her goal of publishing a successful app. She becomes exceptional in a few things rather than average in many things. In fact, she excels in only one powerful skill: coding. And the progress toward her goal is unstoppable.

## Unifying the Principles

I started writing this book assuming that focus is just one of many productivity principles, but it quickly became apparent to me that focus is the unifying principle of all the principles outlined in this book. Let's take a look:

### The 80/20 Principle

Focus on the vital few: remember that 20 percent delivers 80 percent of the results and ignore the trivial many, increasing your productivity by one or two orders of magnitude.

### Build a Minimal Viable Product

Focus on one hypothesis at a time, thereby reducing the complexity of your product, reducing feature creep, and maximizing the rate of progress toward product-market fit. Before you write any line of code, figure out a clear hypothesis about your user's needs. Remove all features except the absolutely necessary. Less is more! Spend more time thinking about what features to implement than actually implementing them. Release your MVP quickly and often, and improve it over time by testing and adding gradually. Use split testing to test the response of two product variants and discard features that don't lead to improvements in key user metrics.

## Write Clean and Simple Code

Complexity slows your understanding of the code and increases the risk of errors. As we learned from Robert C. Martin, "The ratio of time spent reading versus writing is well over 10 to 1. We are constantly reading old code as part of the effort to write new code." Making your code easy to read simplifies the writing of new code. In their famous book *The Elements of Style* (Macmillan, 1959), authors Strunk and White suggest a timeless principle to improve your writing: *omit needless words*. I suggest you extend this principle to programming and *omit needless code*.

## Premature Optimization Is the Root of All Evil

Focus your optimization efforts where they matter. Premature optimization is the act of spending valuable resources on code optimizations that ultimately prove to be unnecessary. As Donald Knuth tells us, "Forget about small efficiencies, say about 97% of the time: premature optimization is the root of all evil." I discussed my top six performance-tuning tips: take metrics for comparisons, consider the 80/20 principle, invest in improving algorithms, apply the less is more principle, cache repeated results, and know when to stop—all of which could be summarized in a single word, *focus*.

## Flow

Flow is a state in which you're completely involved in the task at hand—you're focused and concentrated. Flow researcher Csikszentmihalyi laid out three conditions to achieve flow. (1) Your goals must be clear. Every line of code leads you closer to the successful completion of the larger code project. (2) The feedback mechanism in your environment must be present, and, preferably, immediate. Find people, in person or online, to review your work and follow the MVP principle. (3) There's a balance between opportunity and capacity. If the task is too easy, you'll lose the rush of excitement; if it's too hard, you'll throw in the towel early. If you follow these conditions, you're more likely to achieve a state of pure focus. Ask yourself daily: What can I do *today* to push my software project to the next level? This question is challenging but not overwhelming.

## Do One Thing Well (Unix)

The basic idea of the Unix philosophy is to build simple, clear, concise, modular code that is easy to extend and maintain. This can mean many different things, but the goal is to allow many humans to work together on a codebase by prioritizing human over computer efficiency, favoring composability over monolithic design. You focus every function on one purpose only. You've learned 15 Unix principles to write better code, including small is beautiful, make each function do one thing well, build a prototype as soon as possible, and fail early and noisily. If you keep the *focus* rule at the top of your mind, you'll do just fine in regard to these principles without necessarily needing to memorize every one of them.

### Less Is More in Design

This is about using minimalism to focus your design. Think of the differences between Yahoo Search and Google Search, the Blackberry and the iPhone, and OkCupid and Tinder: the winners are often those technologies with a radically simple user interface. By using a minimalistic web or app design, you focus on the one thing you're doing best. Focus the user's attention on the unique value your product provides!

## Conclusion

Complexity is your enemy because it maximizes entropy. As a builder and creator, you want to minimize entropy: the pure act of creation is one of minimizing entropy. You accomplish this by applying focused effort. Focus is the success secret of every creator. Keep in mind what both Warren Buffett and Bill Gates considered the secret of their success: *focus*.

To implement focus in your work, ask yourself these questions:

- On which software project do I want to focus my efforts?
- Which features do I want to focus on to create my MVP?
- What is the minimal number of design elements I can implement to test the viability of my product?
- Who will use my product and why?
- What can I remove from my code?
- Do my functions do one thing only?
- How can I achieve the same result in less time?

If you keep asking yourself these or similar focusing questions, the money and time you spent on this book have been well worth it.

# LETTER FROM THE AUTHOR

You made it through the whole book, and you've gained insight into how to practically improve your programming skills. You've studied the tactics of writing clean and simple code and the strategies of successful practitioners. Allow me to wrap this book up with a personal note!

Having studied the complexity conundrum, you may ask: If simplification is so powerful, why isn't everybody doing it? The problem is that implementing simplification, despite its great benefits, takes an enormous amount of guts, energy, and willpower. Organizations big and small will often firmly resist removing work and simplifying. Someone was responsible for implementing, maintaining, and managing these features, and they'll often fight tooth and nail to keep their work even if they know it is largely irrelevant. The problem is one of loss aversion—it's hard to let go of anything that provides even the slightest of value. This is something to fight against; I've never regretted any simplification measure I've taken in my life. Pretty much everything has value, but it's important to consider how much you pay for the value you get. When I started my Finxter educational site, I consciously decided to largely ignore social media, and immediately I started to see notable positive results from the additional time I gained to spend on things that move the needle. Simplification is beneficial not just to coding but to all areas of life; it has the power to make your life more efficient and calmer at the same time. Hopefully, by reading this book, you have become more open to simplification, reduction, and focus. If you do decide to follow the route of simplification, you'll be in good company: Albert Einstein believed that "a simple and unassuming manner of life is best for everyone, best both for the body and the mind." Henry David Thoreau concludes: "Simplicity, simplicity, simplicity! I say, let your affairs be as two or three, and not a hundred or a thousand." And Confucius knew that "Life is really simple, but we insist on making it complicated."

To help you with your continuous effort to simplify, I've created a one-page book summary as a Portable Document Format (PDF) that you can download on the book's companion page at *https://blog.finxter.com/simplicity/*, print, and pin to your office wall.

Before you leave, please allow me to express my deep gratitude for you spending so much time with me. My life goal is to help people get more done through code, and I hope this book will help you accomplish that. I hope you have gained insights into how you can boost your coding productivity by doing less. And I hope you start your first, or next, coding project as soon as you turn this page. Cheers toward your success!

# INDEX

colleagues, help with refactoring
from, 77
colors, reducing variations of, 133
comma-separated values (CSV)
format, 110
comments
avoiding unnecessary, 61–63
coding for people, not machines,
56–57
using, 59–61
communication, in defining phase, 5–6
complexity
algorithmic, 8–12
code quality metrics, 76
cognitive, 13
cyclomatic, 12–13, 76
in daily life, 16–17
defined, 4
focus as weapon against, 135–138
in learning, 13–15
methods for solving problem of, 3
in processes, 15–16
in project life cycle, 4–8
simple is better than complex
principle, 106–107
small is beautiful principle, 107
in software, 8–13
sources of, 1–2
unnecessary, 43–44
conditional assignments, 118–119
Confucius, 142
consistency, 58–59, 134
constants, named, 58
continuous deployment, 8
CPU usage, optimizing, 87–88
"Crafting Fun User Experiences: A
Method to Facilitate Flow"
(Schaffer), 97
Csikszentmihalyi, Mihaly, 94, 95, 96,
98–99, 139
CSV (comma-separated values)
format, 110
cyclomatic complexity, 12–13, 76

## D

daily life, complexity in, 16–17
deep work, 16–17

*Deep Work: Rules for Focused Success in a
Distracted World* (Newport), 16
defining phase, complexity in, 5–6
dependencies of code objects,
minimizing, 70–74
deployment phase, complexity in, 8
descriptive names, 57
design elements, removing, 131–132
designing phase, complexity in, 6
design, in MVP generation, 47
design, minimalistic
consistency, 134
design elements, removing, 131–132
features, removing, 132–133
focusing design, 140
fonts and colors, reducing
variations of, 133
material design, 128–129
in mobile phones, 126
in search engines, 127–128
whitespace, using, 129–130
`display_html()` function, 104–105
distractions, avoiding, 16–17, 41, 98
distributed systems, 120
documentation functionality, 63
don't repeat yourself (DRY), 63–65
do one thing well principle, 101,
103–106, 139–140
Dropbox, 46
Drucker, Peter, 97

## E

edit access, 119
efficiency, choosing portability over,
109–110
80/20 principle
in application software
optimization, 21
basics of, 19–20
focus in, 25–27, 138
fractal nature of, 32–34
freelance gigs, 30–32
GitHub repository TensorFlow
contributions, 28–29
implications for coders, 27–32
in performance optimization,
86–88

# RESOURCES

Visit *https://nostarch.com/art-clean-code/* for errata and more information.

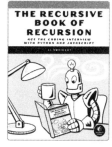

Never before has the world relied so heavily on the Internet to stay connected and informed. That makes the Electronic Frontier Foundation's mission—to ensure that technology supports freedom, justice, and innovation for all people—more urgent than ever.

For over 30 years, EFF has fought for tech users through activism, in the courts, and by developing software to overcome obstacles to your privacy, security, and free expression. This dedication empowers all of us through darkness. With your help we can navigate toward a brighter digital future.